CORINNA KRETSCHMAR-JOEHNK | PETER JOEHNK

RAUM.WERTE.
CREATING HOSPITALITY DESIGN.

▌IMPRINT | IMPRESSUM

The Deutsche Bibliothek is registering this publication in the Deutsche Nationalbibliographie; detailed bibliographical information can be found on the internet at http://dnb.ddb.de

ISBN 978-3-03768-039-1

© 2009 by Braun Publishing AG
www.braun-publishing.ch
1st edition 2009

Concept, text, realisation:
Thomas Schultze, www.schultzeplus.de
Graphic concept and layout:
Heike Schwörer, www.schultzeplus.de
Translation:
Damian Harrison/Network Translators,
(www.networktranslators.de)

CORINNA KRETSCHMAR-JOEHNK | PETER JOEHNK

RAUM.WERTE.
CREATING HOSPITALITY DESIGN.

BRAUN

CONTENTS | INHALT

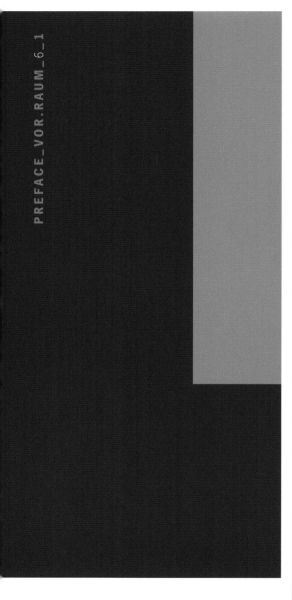

Die Welt scheint außer sich. Jeder im Zustand der Beschleunigung. Es lebe der Transit. Hamburg 12:00 Uhr – Power-napping am Flughafen. London 18:00 Uhr – die Frisur sitzt. Danke Blackberry. Danke Ryanair.

We live in a frenetic world. Everyone seems to be in a state of constant acceleration. Long live rapid transit! Hamburg: 12 o'clock – a quick power-nap at the airport. London: 6:00 p.m. and my hairstyle is still fine. Thank you, Blackberry! Thank you, Ryanair!

Je schneller das Leben wird, desto wichtiger wird – Ankommen. Das Sinnliche und Authentische nimmt an Bedeutung zu, je artifizieller unsere Wirklichkeit erlebt wird. Und wir als Raumgestalter müssen darauf reagieren. Der Wunsch nach Echtem und Unverfälschtem ist dabei mehr als Schein – er ist Sein und quasi überlebenswichtig für alles, was sich jetzt und in Zukunft verkaufen soll.

Denn jeder, der gestalterisch tätig ist, weiß, dass es neben Form vor allem auf die Tragfähigkeit und die Echtheit der Story ankommt, ob etwas Erfolg hat oder nicht. Mehr denn je gilt daher: weg mit Talmi und Tand. Her mit dem Wahren, Schönen, Guten.

Corinna Kretschmar-Joehnk | Manager
Peter Joehnk | Manager

The faster our lives become, the more important it becomes to truly arrive at our destination. The demand for intense, authentic experiences grows as our lives become ever more artificial. It is our responsibility as interior designers to respond to this development. The desire for authentic and unadulterated experiences is anything but superficial – it reflects a state of being and is crucial to the success of quality design, both now and in the future.

Anyone involved in the design industry will tell you that apart from form, it is the credibility and authenticity of a product's story that determine its success or failure. Contemporary design seeks to strip away tinsel and kitsch. Contemporary design is all about the True, the Beautiful and the Good.

This book explores spaces, rooms and ideas. Spaces that succeed in touching us are born from creative ideas that speak directly to our emotions and capture our imagination. We create spaces that are rich in humanity and have something very real to say to us. We strive to design spaces that fulfil visitor's needs and leave a lasting impression.

RAUM.WERTE. | CREATING HOSPITALITY DESIGN. is our first book. We hope to offer our readers an insight into our various projects and highlight the processes underlying successful interior design. Interior design has to be effective, it has to sell and it has to be fun. We invite you to take a look for yourself.

▎PREFACE | VOR.RAUM.

In diesem Buch geht es um Räume und um Ideen. Denn jedem Raum, der uns berührt, liegt eine Schöpfungsidee zugrunde, die uns emotional packt. Wir wollen Räume schaffen, denen Menschlichkeit innewohnt und Räume, die etwas zu erzählen haben. Wir wollen Räume konzipieren, die sich klar an den Bedürfnissen der Besucher orientieren und so nachhaltig Werte schaffen.

RAUM.WERTE. | CREATING HOSPITALITY DESIGN. ist unser erstes Buch. Neben Einblicken in unsere Projekte versuchen wir die Arbeitsprozesse erfolgsorientierter Innenarchitektur deutlich zu machen. Denn Innenarchitektur muss wirken, muss verkaufen und muss Spaß machen. Doch sehen Sie selbst.

DESIGN.TRENDS_INNEN.RAUM_8_2

Design oder nicht sein? Low Price oder Luxus? Wie sieht die Zukunft im Hotelsektor aus? Alles über die Hoteltrends von morgen lesen Sie hier. Jetzt.

To design or not to design? Low price or luxury? What does the future hold for the hotel sector? Read about tomorrow's trends. Here. Now.

DESIGN.TRENDS_INNEN.RAUM

By futurologists
Klaus Burmeister and
Elita Wiegand

Beitrag der Trendforscher
Klaus Burmeister und Elita Wiegand

CREATIVE, FEMININE AND SUSTAINABLE: HOTEL TRENDS 2015 | KREATIV, WEIBLICH UND NACHHALTIG: HOTELTRENDS 2015

Hotels are spaces designed for interaction, communication and relaxation. They reflect the trends, currents and developments that shape our society. It is no surprise that the hotel industry is anything but homogenous. In fact, the industry is defined by its very diversity. Given this fact, are trends in the hotel industry even worth exploring? Yes, simply because hotels have to be open to change. In tomorrow's competitive market for temporary accommodation the personal touch, mind-set and individual character of a hotel will be decisive factors in securing and serving clients, target groups and guests.

Hotels sind exponierte Plätze der Begegnung, des Verweilens und der Kommunikation. Sie sind ein Spiegelbild von Trends, Strömungen und Entwicklungen, die eine Gesellschaft konstituieren. Somit wird eins schon deutlich, ein einheitliches Bild der Hotellandschaft existiert nicht. Vielmehr regiert eine bunte Vielfalt unterschiedlicher Kategorien. Lohnt dann überhaupt ein Blick auf ausgewählte Hoteltrends? Er lohnt, weil sich Hotels den Entwicklungen öffnen müssen. Dabei wird ihre Note, ihre Haltung und Individualität der Garant sein, um ihre Klientel, ihre Zielgruppe, ihre Gäste im umkämpften Markt des temporären Wohnens zu erreichen und zu bedienen.

Trends sind inzwischen Teil der Alltagskultur. Meist sind damit aber kurzfristige Moden gemeint und weniger empirisch nachvollziehbare Entwicklungen. Die folgenden Trends basieren auf einer kontinuierlichen Beschäftigung mit langfristig angelegten Veränderungsdynamiken, die wir als Megatrends bezeichnen.

Megatrends wirken nicht nur in einem gesellschaftlichen Handlungsfeld, sondern sie durchziehen, beeinflussen und verändern die Gesellschaft insgesamt. Ein weiteres Kennzeichen von Megatrends ist, dass sie langfristig (15 Jahre und mehr) und global wirken. Die nachfolgenden Hoteltrends beziehen sich im Kern nur auf Megatrends, von denen wir explizit einen erheblichen Einfluss erwarten. Dazu zählen die Herausbildung wissensbasierter Ökonomien und einer damit einhergehenden Veränderung der Arbeitsphären, die fortschreitende Individualisierung in allen Teilen der Welt, der Vormarsch von Frauen in Wirtschaft und Gesellschaft und last but not least der demographische Wandel, die Digitalisierung aller Lebenswelten und ein nachhaltiger Umgang mit Umwelt und Ressourcen als zentrale Triebkräfte für den Wandel der Hotellandschaften.

Trends have become part of our everyday culture. But the term is generally used to refer to transient phenomena and other developments that are more difficult to track. The following trends are drawn from our ongoing study of long-term processes of transformation. We call these processes "megatrends".

Megatrends are not restricted to disparate social sectors – they will impact on and change our entire society. Megatrends are long-term (15-year) trends with a global reach. The hotel trends described here are based on the megatrends that we expect to impact significantly on our society. These trends include the emergence of knowledge-based economies and the resulting changes to the working world, the continuing global trend towards increasing individualisation, the growing participation of women in our economies and societies, and last but not least, demographic change, the digitalisation of our everyday lives and an increased awareness of the need to use resources in a sustainable manner. These are the driving forces behind the transformation of the hospitality industry.

Was zu erwarten ist:

Die neue Heimat der Kreativen

Flexibel und mobil: Die Attribute stehen für die Business-Wissensnomaden. Für die modernen Knowledgeworker sind Hotels zukünftig wichtige Schnittstellen. In den ortlosen und gesichtslosen Arenen einer globalisierten Weltwirtschaft etablieren sie sich als Gegenpol. Damit unterliegen Hotels einer spannungsreichen Ambivalenz. Temporär angelegt werden sie inspirierende Heimat auf Zeit. Sie können ein Vakuum füllen, in dem sie Menschen als Offline-Begegnungsstätten für Online-Kontakte dienen, als Arbeits- und Lernort, als Projektspace für virtuelle Arbeitsteams sowie als Ruheoasen und Tankstellen für Kreativität. Hotels erleben somit einen Wandel, der ihre bisherige Grundfunktion ergänzt und sich den Erfordernissen der Wissensökonomie anpasst.

Frauen-Power

Vive la Différence. Frauen werden zu einer ökonomisch unverzichtbaren Kraft. Die Wachstumserfordernisse der Weltwirtschaft eröffnen qualifizierten Frauen neue Optionen. Nicht nur durch den demografischen Wandel sind Frauen gefragter denn je. Es sind vor allem die veränderten Anforderungen einer innovationsgetriebenen Wirtschaft, die weibliche Stärken wie Kooperation, Teamarbeit und Kommunikation dringend benötigen. Das neue Selbstbewusstsein der Frauen findet seine Entsprechung in Räumen, Ambiente und Servicekonzepten einer zeitgemäßen Hotelkultur. Es ist eben nicht nur der kleine Unterschied, wie zum Beispiel ein kräftiger Fön, sondern Frauen schätzen eine Wohlfühl-Atmosphäre, eine besondere Ausstrahlung und eine Kultur des Verweilens. Hotels, die sich auf die besonderen Bedürfnisse einstellen, sind für Business-Frauen attraktiv. Der Megatrend wird die Hotels erobern – die weiblichen Gäste sind auf dem Vormarsch.

On the horizon:

New homes for creative professionals

Flexibility and mobility: these two words capture the spirit of the knowledge economy's professional nomads. Hotels are vital interfaces for modern knowledge workers. Hotels are set to establish themselves as an opposite pole to the bleak and impersonal arenas of the global world economy. A tense ambivalence underlies this development. Designed for short term usage, they will become inspiring temporary homes. A hotel can fill a vacuum: as an off-line meeting place for on-line contacts, or as a place to study and work. A hotel can be a workspace for virtual teams and an oasis of tranquillity, a place to replenish your creative spirit. In the coming transformation hotels will expand their repertoire of services as they adapt to the culture and needs of the knowledge-based economy.

Women on the move

Vive la différence! Women are becoming an indispensible power in the working world. The growth of the global economy is creating new opportunities for well-qualified women. But it's not just demographic change that is driving this trend. The global economy is powered by innovation – a fact that has increased the demand for "feminine" soft skills such as the ability to cooperate, along with team-working and communication skills. The growing confidence and strength of contemporary women is reflected in the rooms, atmosphere and service concepts of cutting edge hotels. It's not just the little things like more powerful hairdryers that make a difference – women appreciate an atmosphere of well-being and comfort, a special ambience, and a culture of rest and relaxation. Hotels that adapt to this new demand will be especially attractive for businesswomen. The megatrends are conquering the hotel industry – and female guests are on the move.

Sustainable pleasure

LOHAS (Lifestyles of Health and Sustainability) are at the forefront of a trend that will significantly alter both our society and the global economy. LOHAS represent a fundamental change that will transform our relationship with the environment. LOHAS are not just a fad or a transient expression of our zeitgeist. Sustainability is not about ideology. Rather, the focus is on the development of low-impact lifestyles and approaches to building, energy consumption and food production. This new way of life is reflected in new forms of pleasure. Its success will be marked not by a trend towards frugality but by the emergence of a new design language that translates style, sensuality, quality, values, wellness and health into new hospitality concepts.

Community building

How do clients find a hotel that suits their individual needs? Finding suitable accommodation can be a long and torturous process. In the future individual operators and industry associations will move to help clients locate their services by building communities through social networks such as XING or Facebook. These online communities will therefore play a key role in the success of the hotels of tomorrow. Open approaches to innovation will also have a significant effect on the hospitality industry. Personal recommendation marketing and the establishment of an interactive dialogue that enables clients to actively participate in the design of hotel environments are essential features of an emerging model of cooperative "social commerce". The most successful hotels of tomorrow will most likely function as communities in their own right.

Nachhaltig genießen

Die LOHAS (Lifestyle of Health and Sustainability) sind die Vorboten einer sich nachhaltig verändernden Wirtschaft und Gesellschaft. Es geht nicht um Moden oder um Zeitgeist, sondern um ein grundsätzliches Umsteuern, das künftig unser Verhältnis zur Natur bestimmt. Es geht nicht um Ideologie, sondern um einen lebenspraktischen Umgang mit Energie, Bauen und Wohnen, Essen und Leben. Dieser Lebensstil findet seine Entsprechung in neuen Formen des Genusses. Nicht Verzichtsforderungen werden den Erfolg begleiten, vielmehr eine eigene Sprache, die Stil und Sinnlichkeit, Qualität und Werte, Wohlfühlen und Gesundheit in neuartige Hotelkonzepte übersetzt.

Community Building

Wie findet der Gast das Hotel seiner ganz persönlichen Wahl? Heute ist es oft eine Tortur, bis man etwas Passendes gefunden hat. Zukünftig wird es für Hotels ein zentraler Erfolgsfaktor sein, dem Community erprobten Gast das Finden zu erleichtern. Dazu wird es nötig sein, sich selbst als Mitglied und auch im Verbund mit anderen Hotels in Communities à la XING oder Facebook einzuklinken. Open Innovation-Ansätze werden auch das Gastgewerbe nachhaltig prägen. Empfehlungsmarketing und eine intensive Interaktion mit den Gästen, die es ihnen ermöglicht, ihre Hotel-Lebenswelten mitzugestalten, prägen das Leitbild eines kooperativen „Social Commerce". Das erfolgreiche Hotel der Zukunft ist im besten Fall selbst eine Community.

Other developments

We can expect to see further increases in social polarity as pressure on the middle classes continues to grow. Innovative budget hotels have every opportunity of meeting with success. Reduce to the max, cheap becomes chic – we only need to recall the Swatch watch. The premium customer segment will continue to thrive, but will face ever more demanding customer expectations. As competition grows, it will get tougher at the top.

It might sound old-fashioned, but a renaissance of owner-operated hotels might well be on the horizon. People appreciate the personal style and unique culture of hospitality that pervade owner-operated hotels. You only have to take a sideways glance at the corporate world to see that it is the "small players" who are willing to pioneer risky innovations. The hotel industry is no exception. Demand for specialised services is set to grow, but will continue to be limited to small target groups. Hotels can respond to this trend by entering into cooperative partnerships or introducing new approaches to diversification.

Was weiterhin erwartet werden darf, ...

Die Polarisierung in der Gesellschaft und der Druck auf die Mittelschicht wird anhalten. Billighotels der neuen Art haben Chancen. Reduce to the max, billig wird chic, erinnern wir uns nur an die Swatch-Uhren. Auf der anderen Seite wird das Premium-Kundensegment auf hohem Niveau verharren, allerdings bei weiter steigenden Ansprüchen. Oben wird die Luft noch dünner und die Konkurrenz tendenziell größer.

Fast altmodisch mag es anmuten, aber die Renaissance von Inhaber geführten Hotels ist zu erwarten. Sie machen den entscheidenden Unterschied, ihre individuelle Handschrift prägt die Kultur der Hotels und das spüren die Gäste. Risikoreiche Innovationen im Hotelmetier sind, das zeigt nicht zuletzt der Blick in die internationale Konzernwelt, auch eher von den „Kleinen" zu erwarten. Die weitere Ausdifferenzierung individueller Kundenwünsche bleibt ein durchgehender Trend, allerdings für jeweils sehr überschaubare Zielgruppen. Hotels können entweder durch Kooperationen oder durch neue Konzepte der Multidiversifizierung darauf reagieren.

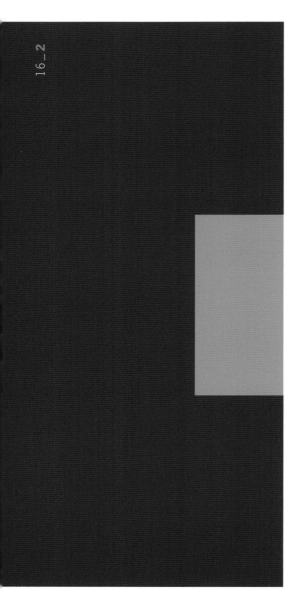

A commitment to mobile broadband networking technologies and the potentials of Web 2.0 – soon to be followed by Web 3.0 (the network of things) – will make hotels increasingly attractive locations for knowledge-workers. The growing ubiquity of broadband technologies allows professionals to work in settings that fulfil their personal needs for relaxation, communication and meaning – in other words, environments that address both aspects of our being.

Intelligent and efficient energy management will be a further hallmark of the stylish and forward-looking hotels of the future.

Looking ahead

Trends come and go, and target groups reinvent themselves as new needs and desires emerge. The only constant factor is change itself. Hoteliers will need to closely monitor their target groups and communities in order to meet their clients' constantly changing needs. By thinking ahead, considering alternatives and employing strategic management hoteliers will be able to plan their investments effectively. Successful hotels will be able to identify, assess and implement emerging trends at an early stage.

Erst eine intensive Nutzung mobiler, breitbandiger Netztechnologien, verbunden mit den Möglichkeiten des Web 2.0 sowie dann 3.0 (Netz der Dinge), macht Hotels für die Wissensarbeiter zu attraktiven Orten. Sie ermöglichen die Vereinbarkeit von Arbeit mit den individuellen Bedürfnissen nach Ruhe, Sinn und Kommunikation als beide Seiten ihrer Existenz.

Eine intelligente und energieeffiziente Energieversorgung und -steuerung wird darüber hinaus ein zukunftsfähiges und smartes Hotel auszeichnen.

Ausblick

Trends kommen und gehen, Zielgruppen verändern sich, und neue Wünsche und Bedürfnisse entstehen fast in Echtzeit. Nur der Wandel ist konstant. Hoteliers werden auf die Kontinuität des Wandels mit einem systematischen und kontinuierlichen Monitoring ihrer Zielgruppen und Umfelder reagieren müssen. Frühzeitig vorbereitet zu sein, ein Denken in Alternativen und strategisches Handeln hilft bei notwendigen Investitionsentscheidungen. Erfolgreichen Hotels gelingt es, Trends rechtzeitig zu erkennen, zu bewerten und angemessen umzusetzen.

Klaus Burmeister
Geschäftsführer

Klaus Burmeister ist Gründer und geschäftsführender Gesellschafter von Z_punkt und verantwortet Innovations- und Foresightprozesse für namhafte Unternehmen. Der gelernte Starkstromelektriker war nach seinem Studium der Politologie lange Jahre als Wissenschaftler an der Freien Universität Berlin, am Institut für Zukunftsstudien und Technologiebewertung (IZT) sowie am Sekretariat für Zukunftsforschung (SFZ) tätig.

Elita Wiegand
Geschäftsführerin

Elita Wiegand ist Gründerin von „innovativ-in", dem Businessclub für Wertschöpfer, Innovatoren und Querdenker, Journalistin und Chefredakteurin von „business-on" – dem regionalen Online-Magazin und Geschäftsführerin der e-lita GmbH. Sie beschäftigt sich seit Jahren mit der Frage, wie Innovation in Wirtschaft und Gesellschaft erfolgreich verankert werden können.

Klaus Burmeister
Managing Director

Klaus Burmeister is the founder and managing director of Z_punkt, a specialist company that manages innovation and foresight processes for prestigious corporate clients. A trained high-voltage electrician, Klaus Burmeister majored in political science and has conducted research at Berlin's Freie Universität, at the Institute for Future Studies and Technology Assessment (IZT) and at the Sekretariat für Zukunftsforschung (SFZ – Secretariat for Future Studies).

Elita Wiegand
Managing Director

Elita Wiegand is the founder of "innovativ-in", a business club for value generators, innovative thinkers and creative minds, and the managing director of e-lita GmbH. As a journalist and chief editor of the regional online magazine "business-on", Elita Wiegand is an expert on the delivery and incorporation of innovative change within the economy and society.

Klaus Burmeister | Managing Director
Elita Wiegand | Managing Director

Zuhören. Analysieren. Scribbeln. Entwerfen. Verwerfen. Begreifen. Raumgestaltung ist Arbeit. Jedes Projekt ist anders. Jedes hat seine Geschichte.

Listen. Analyse. Scribble. Draft. Scrap. Comprehend. Interior design is work. Every project is different. And every project has its own history.

DESIGN.PROJECTS_PROJEKT.RAUM

AUFGABE

Welch Geschichte! Der Gutshof aus dem Jahr 1556 wurde bereits einmal komplett demontiert, in Container eingelagert und wartete auf seine Verschiffung in die USA. Dort sollte er als Symbol deutscher Gemütlichkeit gastronomisch genutzt werden. Vor 20 Jahren fand der Gutshof dann seine neue Heimat in Großburgwedel und wird seither als Hotel genutzt. Aufgabe war der Komplettumbau des Gutshauses unter Berücksichtigung der historischen Bausubstanz. Kurzum: Neues sollte entstehen, ohne dass das Alte negiert wird.

LÖSUNG

In einem sensiblen Dialog zwischen Historie und Moderne wurde die komplette Raumstruktur geändert. Offene Raumstrukturen schaffen dabei überraschende Durchblicke und geben eine klare Orientierung. Das Design ist reduziert auf ruhige, kraftvolle Flächen, die in Glas und Mooreiche Geschichte und Moderne widerspiegeln. Die Farben beschränken sich auf weiß und dunkelbraun – horizontale Flächen sind in Crèmetönen gehalten.

ERGEBNIS

Die kraftvolle Hülle eines Bauernhauses bildet den Rahmen für moderne Einbauten, wobei sich durch den Kontrast sowohl das zeitgemäße Design als auch die historische Substanz in ihrer Wirkung gegenseitig steigern.

THE BRIEF

What a magnificent history! Constructed in 1556, this grand farmhouse was later dismantled and packed into shipping containers bound for the USA, where it was to be reborn as a restaurant infused with German gemütlichkeit. The house eventually found a new home in Grossburgwedel twenty years ago and has been used as a hotel ever since. Our task was to completely renovate the house while preserving its historical substance. To put it in a nutshell: our job was to create, not negate.

THE SOLUTION

We remodelled the entire spatial structure in a sensitive dialogue between modern architecture and the building's inspiring history. In the process we created generous open spaces and astonishing views, while facilitating spatial orientation. The design emphasises the powerful glass and bog oak surfaces, simultaneously reflecting the structure's history and modernity. The color scheme is limited to white and dark brown tones, while horizontal surfaces are presented in cream tones.

HOTEL KOKENHOF | GROSSBURGWEDEL

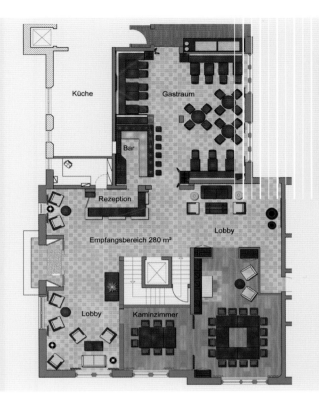

CATEGORY | KATEGORIE
4*

THE BRIEF | AUFGABE
Total renovation and restructuring of public areas |
Komplettrenovierung und Neustrukturierung Public Areas

SIZE | GRÖSSE
980 m²

HOTEL TYPE | HOTEL-TYP
Business/conference hotel | Business-/Konferenzhotel

PROJECT COMPLETED IN | BAUJAHR
2005

COMPLETION PERIOD | BAUZEIT
2 months | 2 Monate

THE RESULT

A farmhouse's powerful exterior presents an ideal
context for a modern interior. The visual contrast
heightens the effect of the contemporary design and the
historical structure.

COMMENTS

The combination of a new interior in an old shell is
proving to be a success for the operators of the
Kokenhof Hotel. The design has been well received by
clients that are otherwise less attuned to modern
interior design and the operators have seen revenues
grow following refurbishment.

STIMMEN

Neues Design in alter Hülle
scheint für den Betreiber zu einem
Erfolgskonzept zu werden, denn
das Gebäude schlägt die Brücke zu
Menschen, die mitunter keinen
Zugang zu moderner Formensprache
haben. Seit dem Umbau verzeichnet
der Bauherr steigende Umsätze.

HOTEL KOKENHOF | GROSSBURGWEDEL

1

2

1 | Kontaktaufnahme: Ein hinterleuchteter Empfangstresen lädt Gäste ein.
2 | Vor dem Umbau: Der massive Empfangsbereich vermittelt kaum Offenheit.

1 | Inviting contact: A backlit reception desk draws guests into the lobby.
2 | Before refurbishment: The wood-panelled reception area failed to communicate a sense of openness.

HOTEL KOKENHOF | GROSSBURGWEDEL

| | | | | | | | | | | | | | | | | | | | | | | | | | | |

1 | "Wunderbar": Light is a central element of the Kokenhof's design. The delicately backlit bar fills the room with a pleasant level of background lighting.
2 | Setting the mood: The cornice lighting and wall lamps in the restaurant create a pleasantly reserved lighting scheme. An antique wagon wheel separates the restaurant area from the rest of the building.
3 | The restaurant prior to refurbishment: Lots of wood, but little warmth.

1 | Wunderbar: Licht ist eines der zentralen Gestaltungselemente im Kokenhof. Der hinterleuchtete Tresen sorgt für eine angenehme Grundhelligkeit.
2 | Stimmungsmacher: Im Restaurantbereich ist das Licht aus den Vouten und Wandleuchten angenehm zurückhaltend. Ein archaisches Rad trennt den Restaurantbereich.
3 | Restaurantbereich vor dem Umbau: Viel Holz, aber keine Wärme.

1+2 | A stunning transformation: The conference zone bar.
3 | The face of yesterday: The bar with beer taps.

1+2 | Wandelbar: Die Bar zum
Konferenzbereich.
3 | Blick in die Vergangenheit:
Tresen mit Zapfhahn.

1 | The fireplace prior
to renovation.
2 | Earth tones: Solid wood
furniture upholstered with
naturally tanned leather
furniture.
3 | The fireplace: Guests can
relax in a cosy armchair at the
fireside. Warm shades
dominate the restaurant.

1 | Der Kaminbereich vor
dem Umbau.
2 | Erdig gut: Naturgegerb-
tes Leder und Vollholzmöbel
im Restaurantbereich.
3 | Feuerquelle: In groß-
zügigen Sesseln entspannen
die Gäste vor dem Kamin.
Im Restaurantbereich
dominieren warme Töne.

HOTEL KOKENHOF | GROSSBURGWEDEL

MÖVENPICK HOTEL | MUNICH AIRPORT | MÜNCHEN AIRPORT

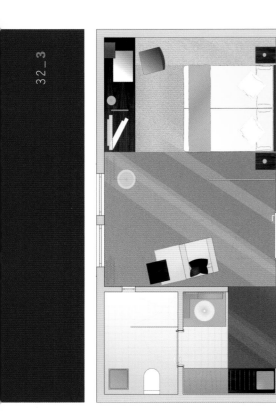

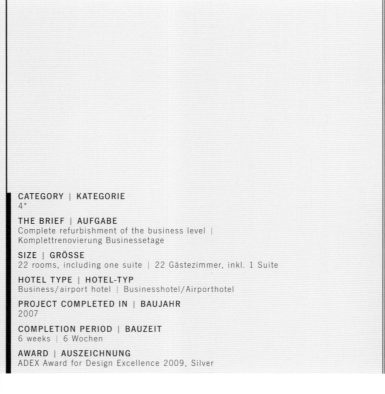

CATEGORY | KATEGORIE
4*

THE BRIEF | AUFGABE
Complete refurbishment of the business level |
Komplettrenovierung Businessetage

SIZE | GRÖSSE
22 rooms, including one suite | 22 Gästezimmer, inkl. 1 Suite

HOTEL TYPE | HOTEL-TYP
Business/airport hotel | Businesshotel/Airporthotel

PROJECT COMPLETED IN | BAUJAHR
2007

COMPLETION PERIOD | BAUZEIT
6 weeks | 6 Wochen

AWARD | AUSZEICHNUNG
ADEX Award for Design Excellence 2009, Silver

THE BRIEF

Our task was to completely renovate a suite and one level of guest accommodation at the Mövenpick Hotel Munich Airport. The project's primary goal was to enhance the well-being and comfort of hotel guests by creating an inspiring and relaxed atmosphere for travellers arriving from Munich Airport.

AUFGABE

Für das Mövenpick Hotel München Airport sollten eine Gästezimmeretage und eine Suite komplett renoviert werden. Übergeordnetes Ziel des Umbaus war eine Erhöhung des Erholungsfaktors für den Gast. Der Reisende – eben noch im Flieger – soll im Hotel schnell entspannen und in inspirierender Atmosphäre arbeiten können.

LÖSUNG

Hereinspaziert Natur! Das Designkonzept trägt den Titel „Outside In". Natürliche Elemente setzen einen Gegenpol zur hochtechnisierten Welt des Flughafens. Piniengrüne Wände stehen neben sandfarbenen Fliesen und warmen Holztönen. Die Formensprache ist zurückhaltend und geradlinig, sie lässt die Materialien durch ihre Texturen und Oberflächen wirken und die Farben in feinsten Abstufungen nebeneinander strahlen.

THE SOLUTION

Welcome to nature! The design concept is titled "Outside In". The natural elements of the design form an inspiring antithesis to the airport's high-tech environs. Pine green walls compliment the sand-colored tiles and the warm tones of the wood. The reserved use of form enables the materials to speak with their textures and surfaces, and accentuates the delicate color scheme of the rooms.

THE RESULT

The business level welcomes its guests with a fresh, warm ambience and sensitive color composition.

ERGEBNIS

In der Businessetage entstand ein frisches und zugleich warmes Ambiente, das durch seine sensible Farbkomposition besticht.

1

1 | Sylvan style: A translucent fabric printed with a sylvan design separates the different sections of the room.
2 | A flash of light: The pendulum lamps underscore the light, floating style of the work zone and the bedside table.
3 | The flow of color: Green is used on furniture undersides and interiors to influence mood, essentially prefiguring the all-green bathroom.

1 | Waldarbeit: Ein transluzenter Stoff mit Astmuster trennt die Bereiche im Raum.
2 | Lichtblick: Die Pendelleuchten neben dem Bett betonen den schwebenden Charakter von Arbeitsplatz und Nachttischen.
3 | „Outside In": Die Akzentfarbe Grün findet sich in Möbelunter- oder Innenseiten – quasi eine Vorankündigung für das ganz in grün gehaltene Bad.

MÖVENPICK HOTEL | MUNICH AIRPORT | MÜNCHEN AIRPORT

1 | Grüne Welle: Das Bad empfängt den Reisenden in knackigem Apfelgrün.
2 | Lichtes Laub: Glasflächen unterstreichen Frische und schenken den Oberflächen zugleich Tiefe.
3 | Grüne Oase: Das Grün der Wände wird bei Glasmosaik und Waschtisch aufgenommen.

1 | Green wave: The bathroom greets visitors with a crisp green apple tone.
2 | A leafy haven: The glass surfaces evoke a fresh atmosphere and add depth to the rooms.
3 | A green oasis: The green wall tones are reflected in the glass mosaic and the bathroom console.

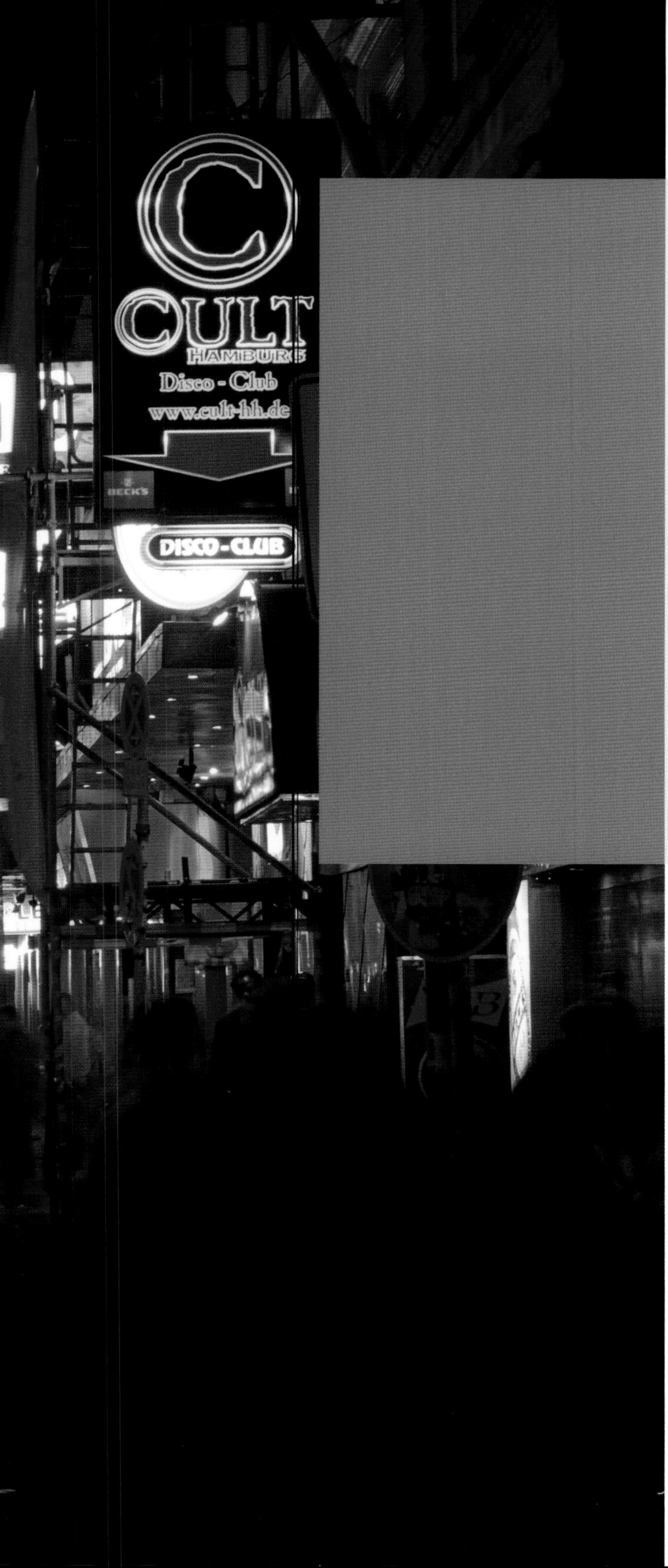
C
CULT
HAMBURG
Disco - Club
www.cult-hh.de
BECK'S
DISCO-CLUB

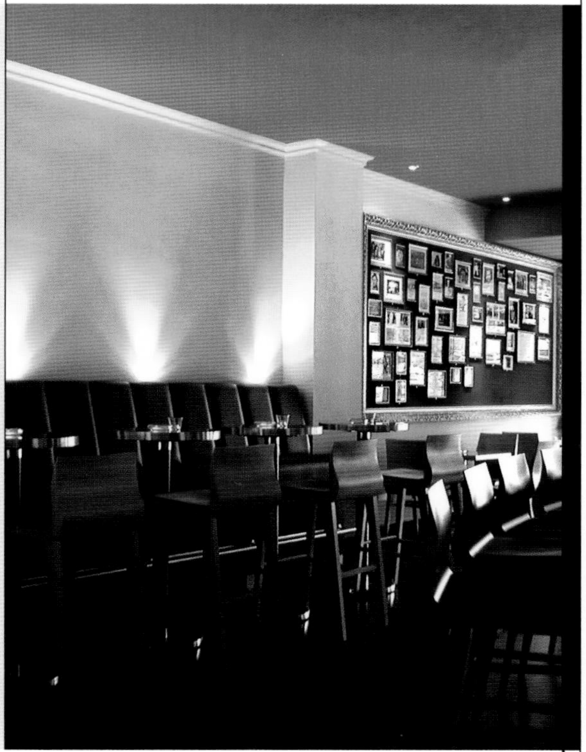

THE BRIEF

The City Hotel Monopol is located on Hamburg's Reeperbahn. The project entailed the full renovation of the bar and restaurant of this well-known hotel. The challenge: To develop a contemporary design that attracts new customers without disappointing the hotel's regular clients.

THE SOLUTION

A blend of baroque elements and Hanseatic integrity.

THE RESULT

From the pop band Die Prinzen to Otto Sander, Helge Schneider and Hildegard Knef, guests and visitors have long adored the Monopol Hotel. And now it's more popular than ever!

AUFGABE

Direkt an Hamburgs Reeperbahn liegt das City Hotel Monopol. In der bekannten Künstlerherberge sollte der Bar- und Restaurantbereich umgebaut werden. Die Herausforderungen: Stammgäste nicht vergraulen und neue Gäste durch zeitgemäßes Ambiente gewinnen.

LÖSUNG

Barocke Elemente treffen auf hanseatische Geradlinigkeit.

ERGEBNIS

Die Prinzen, Otto Sander, Helge Schneider, Hildegard Knef – Gäste und Besucher lieben das Monopol. Und nach dem Umbau mehr denn je.

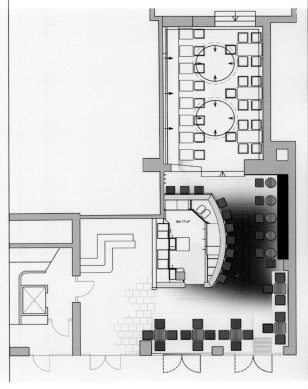

CATEGORY | KATEGORIE
3*

THE BRIEF | AUFGABE
Total renovation of bar and restaurant area |
Komplettrenovierung Bar und Gastronomieflächen

SIZE | GRÖSSE
115 m²

HOTEL TYPE | HOTEL-TYP
City hotel/cult art hotel in St. Pauli | Stadthotel/
Künstler- und Kulthotel auf St. Pauli

PROJECT COMPLETED IN | BAUJAHR
2005

COMPLETION PERIOD | BAUZEIT
2 weeks | 2 Wochen

1

HOTEL MONOPOL | HAMBURG

2

1 | The bar: The mosaic pillar and backlit bar set a sophisticated tone.
2 | Light moments: This striking ribbon of light gives the bar an ephemeral, floating character. The circular ceiling details and reserved lighting create an intimate atmosphere in the restaurant.

1 | Anlaufstelle: Eine mit Mosaiksteinen geflieste Säule. Die Bar setzt mit dem hinterleuchteten Barblatt einen edlen Akzent.
2 | Lichte Momente: Die Bar erscheint durch einen Lichtstreifen am Sockel schwebend. Im Restaurantteil markieren kreisrunde Deckenausschnitte mit gedämpftem Licht den ruhigen Bereich.

1

2

1 | A warm ambience: Smoked oak and wengé are combined with milk-coffee colored walls, rich bordeaux and orange tones to create a warm atmosphere.
2 | The modern chandeliers in the front section of the bar.

1 | Warme Sache: Räuchereiche und Wenge wurden mit milchkaffeefarbenen Wänden und sattem Bordeauxrot und Orange kombiniert.
2 | Moderne Kronleuchter im vorderen Bereich der Bar.

THE BRIEF
This project entailed the conversion of the former executive casino into a restaurant for private functions at the 5-star Le Royal Méridien Hotel in Hamburg. A suitable name was also required for the new restaurant.

THE SOLUTION
The eighth floor of the Le Royal Méridien Hotel is as close as you can get to heaven in Hamburg, so it seemed only natural to name the new restaurant "Le Soleil" – a perfect companion to the existing "Le Ceil" restaurant.

AUFGABE
Für das 5-Sterne Hotel Le Royal Méridien in Hamburg sollte das ehemalige Vorstandscasino im Nachbargebäude zu einem Restaurant für geschlossene Gesellschaften umgebaut werden. Zudem wurde ein Name für das neue Restaurant gesucht.

LÖSUNG
Im 8. Stock des Le Royal Méridien ist man dem Himmel ziemlich nah. Folglich wurde der Restaurantbereich „Le Soleil" genannt. Zusammen mit dem bestehenden „Le Ciel" bilden zwei Restaurants jetzt ein Traumpaar.

THE RESULT

The focus of the color and material scheme is on warm natural tones, with accents in orange and light blue. The use of form in the new restaurant blends in well with the clear, linear structures found elsewhere in the hotel. Sliding walls of fine hardwood can be employed to separate the buffet zone from the remainder of the restaurant.

ERGEBNIS

Warme Naturtöne bilden die Basis für das Farb- und Materialkonzept. Akzente werden gesetzt durch Orange und Hellblau. Geradlinige Strukturen schließen an die Formensprache des Hotels an. Schiebewände aus edlem Holz trennen bei Bedarf den Buffetbereich ab.

CATEGORY | KATEGORIE
Fine dining restaurant in 5* hotel |
Gourmetrestaurant in 5* Hotel

THE BRIEF | AUFGABE
Design and construction of an
additional restaurant for events |
Einbau eines zusätzlichen
Restaurants für Veranstaltungen

SIZE | GRÖSSE
310 m²

HOTEL TYPE | HOTEL-TYP
City hotel | Stadthotel

PROJECT COMPLETED IN | BAUJAHR
2005

COMPLETION PERIOD | BAUZEIT
5 weeks | 5 Wochen

RESTAURANT „LE SOLEIL", LE ROYAL MERIDIEN | HAMBURG

1 | Solar power: This glass panel featuring an etching of sunrays divides the entrances to the conference and guest areas.

2 | A warm welcome: The light installation and etching transforms the glass wall bordering the restaurant into an eye-catching feature.

1 | Sonnenkraft: Eine Glasscheibe mit eingeätzten Sonnenstrahlen trennt den Zugang zum Konferenzbereich vom Gastbereich.

2 | Warmer Empfang: Die Glaswand bildet den räumlichen Abschluss des Restaurants und stellt durch eine innen liegende Beleuchtung einen schönen Blickfang dar.

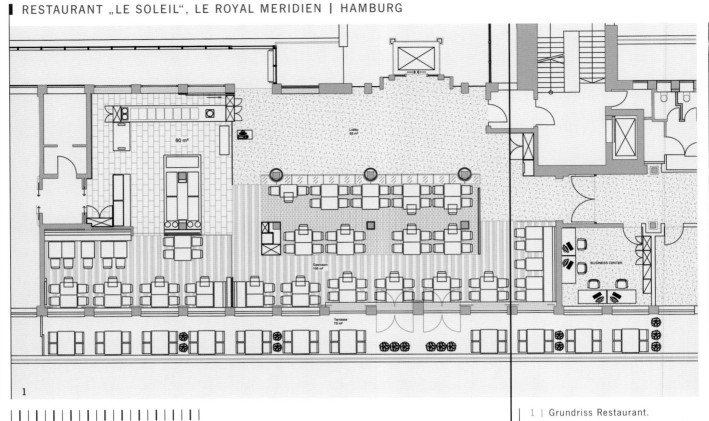

1

| | | | | | | | | | | | | | | | | | | | | | | | | | |

1 | Restaurant floor plan.
2 | Woven designs:
Woven leather furnishings
underscore the restaurant's
sophisticated style.
3 | Rear-view mirror: Guests
seated with their backs to the
windows still enjoy a panoramic
view of the Alster Lake thanks
to these ingenious mirrors.

1 | Grundriss Restaurant.
2 | Flechtwerk: Geflochtenes Leder
unterstreicht den edlen Charakter
des Gesamtkonzeptes.
3 | Rückspiegel: Gäste, die mit
dem Rücken zum Fenster sitzen,
müssen dank raffiniert angebrachter
Spiegel nicht auf das Alster-
panorama verzichten.

2

3

THE BRIEF

The unique design of this café (later named the mini bar) in the lobby of the City Hotel Hanover enables it to operate as a coffee bar by day and a cocktail bar by night.

THE SOLUTION

The bar furnishings, featuring kitchen cabinets and backlit bar shelving, are suitable for use around the clock. The color scheme ranges from red through to brown, and features black and white accents. The warm yellow tone rounds off the color composition and sets off the bar.

AUFGABE

Am Tag sollte die Lobby des City Hotels in Hannover, die später den Namen mini bar erhielt, als Coffee Shop und abends als Cocktailbar genutzt werden.

LÖSUNG

Ein Barmöbel mit Kuchenvitrine und einem hinterleuchteten Flaschendisplay gewährleisten Einsatz bei Tag und bei Nacht. Das Farbspektrum reicht von Rot über Braun bis hin zu schwarz-weißen Akzenten. Warmes Gelb rundet das Farbspiel ab und setzt die Bar in Szene.

MINI BAR | HANOVER | HANNOVER

MINI BAR | HANOVER | HANNOVER

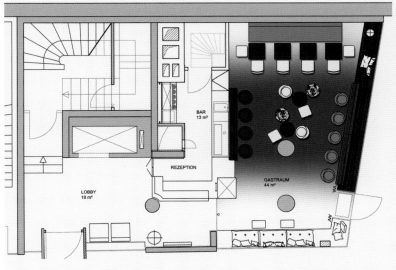

CATEGORY | KATEGORIE
3*

THE BRIEF | AUFGABE
Complete refurbishment of the hotel
lobby and inclusion of a new bar |
Komplettrenovierung Hotellobby mit
Einbau einer Bar

SIZE | GRÖSSE
76 m²

HOTEL TYPE | HOTEL-TYP
City hotel | Stadthotel

PROJECT COMPLETED IN | BAUJAHR
2006

COMPLETION PERIOD | BAUZEIT
1 month | 1 Monat

The café's high ceilings are emphasised by the use of a
red tone suitably matched to the bright red benches.
Massive chandeliers accentuate the visual design and form
an eye-catching feature for passers-by. The stylish modern
chandeliers and wallpapering invoke historical designs and
build a bridge to the present.

Die hohen Räumlichkeiten werden
unterstrichen durch eine rote Decke,
die mit einer überhohen knallroten
Sitzbank korrespondiert. Riesige
Kronleuchter akzentuieren und bilden
den Blickfang für Passanten von
außen. Neu definierte Kronleuchter
und Tapeten zitieren die Vergangen-
heit und bauen eine Brücke in die
Gegenwart.

CATEGORY | KATEGORIE
4* superior

THE BRIEF | AUFGABE
Total renovation of four floors of a historical
"Bäderstil" villa | Komplettrenovierung einer
Bäderstilvilla auf 4 Ebenen

SIZE | GRÖSSE
900 m²

HOTEL TYPE | HOTEL-TYP
Medical wellness: Concept artepuri
med center | Medical Wellness:
Konzept artepuri med center

PROJECT COMPLETED IN | BAUJAHR
2006

COMPLETION PERIOD | BAUZEIT
3 months | 3 Monate

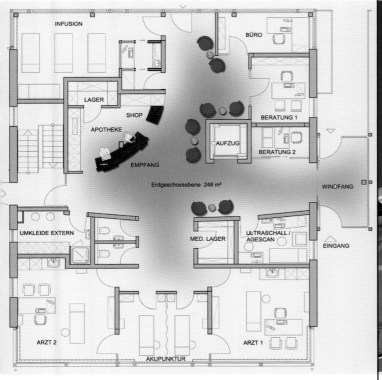

THE BRIEF

Rügen. Chalk cliffs. The Baltic Sea. Hotel meerSinn decided to extend its range of wellness and healthcare services by opening a new center for preventive, regenerative and holistic medicine in the neighbouring 900-square-meter "Bäderstil" villa. The challenge: To preserve the hotel's historical substance while simultaneously creating a modern design.

THE SOLUTION

Regionally sourced materials dominate the visual design, while the color composition and lighting reflect the island's frequently changing light conditions.

THE RESULT

The artepuri med center, which is unique in Germany, has become an established presence on Rügen. The hotel has benefited from this development: meerSinn is now a leading player in the national and international four-star superior segment.

AUFGABE

Rügen. Kreidefelsen. Ostsee. Das Hotel meerSinn wollte sein Spektrum auf dem Wellness-Sektor mit einem neuartigen Gesundheitsangebot erweitern. In der angrenzenden Bäderstilvilla sollte ein Zentrum für präventive und regenerative Ganzheitsmedizin auf über 900 m² entstehen. Die Herausforderung: Die Geschichte des Hotels wahren und den Sprung in die Moderne wagen.

LÖSUNG

Materialien aus der Region bilden die gestalterische Klammer. Farb- und Lichtstimmungen lehnen sich an die schnell wechselnden Lichtverhältnisse der Insel an.

ERGEBNIS

Das in Deutschland einzigartige artepuri med center ist zu einer festen Größe auf Rügen geworden. Davon profitiert auch das Hotel: Das meerSinn hat sich zu einem der führenden Häuser im 4-Sterne superior Segment auf nationaler und internationaler Ebene etabliert.

artepuri

1

2

1 | Playing with colors: The gently shifting colors of this nine-meter-high lighting stele make it the key feature of the four-story atrium.

2 | Two strong vertical elements dominate the central light well, which connects with all of the center's rooms.

3 | Time out: Like all of the center's treatment areas this relaxation room features parquet flooring in native beechwood.

1 | Farbspiel: Eine 9 m hohe Lichtstele ändert sanft die Farbe und wird so zum zentralen Blickfang des viergeschossigen Atriums.

2 | In dem zentralen Lichthof, über den sich alle Räume erschließen, prägen zwei starke vertikale Elemente den Raum.

3 | Auszeit: Im Ruheraum, wie in allen anderen Behandlungsräumen, wurde Parkettbodenbelag aus heimischer Buche gewählt.

ARTEPURI MED CENTER | BINZ, RÜGEN

1

1 | Wasser treten: Die sandfarbenen Fliesen erinnern an den Sandstrand der nahe gelegenen Ostsee.
2 | Naturspiele: Die Dekoration wurde mit Mareile Hellwig gestaltet. Federn, Strand, Treibgut, Gräser sind die poetischen Elemente der Bilder, Skulpturen und Dekorationen.

1 | Treading water: The sand-colored tiles are reminiscent of the nearby beaches.
2 | Natural design: This decorative element was co-designed by Mareile Hellwig. Feathers, beach, flotsam and grass are the poetic elements of the center's paintings, sculptures and decorative installations.

ARTEPURI MED CENTER | BINZ, RÜGEN

THE BRIEF

Ageing splendour in the heart of a
pulsating metropolis: Since its
establishment in the early twentieth
century, Le Méridien Parkhotel
has provided an enchanting oasis for
its guests on Frankfurt's Wiesenhüttenplatz. The challenge: To create
a contemporary interior design that
revitalises the hotel, while retaining
regular customers and preserving
Le Méridien's unique style.

AUFGABE

Alte Pracht trifft auf pulsierende Großstadt: Das
Le Méridien Parkhotel am Wiesenhüttenplatz in Frankfurt
am Main verzaubert seine Gäste seit Beginn des
20. Jahrhunderts. Die Herausforderungen: Die Innenaus-
stattung neu planen, Stammgäste halten, neuen Zeitgeist
einziehen lassen, den alten Hausgeist bewahren.

LÖSUNG

Klassisches Ambiente im Mix mit modernem Design.
Die kräftige Bausubstanz mit ihrer spürbaren Geschichte
gab den Rahmen vor. Die neuen Elemente sind im
Kontrast dazu modern eingesetzt.

ERGEBNIS

Das Hotel stellt jetzt eine perfekte Symbiose aus
klassischem Grand Hotel und trendorientiertem Lifestyle-
Hotel dar. Es entsteht eine angenehme Spannung, die aber
nie Gefahr läuft, dass das neue Parkhotel zerrissen würde
zwischen dem Gestern und Heute.

THE SOLUTION

Classical ambience complimented by
modern design. The hotel's robust
historical architecture sets the context.
New elements have been applied with a
modern flair, creating a contrast
between the past and present.

THE RESULT

The hotel is a perfect symbiosis of the
classical Grand Hotel and contemporary
trend-oriented lifestyle hotels. The
aesthetic tension of the design is palpable
and exciting. The play of "yesterday" and
"today" that characterises the new Park
Hotel is thoughtful and sophisticated.

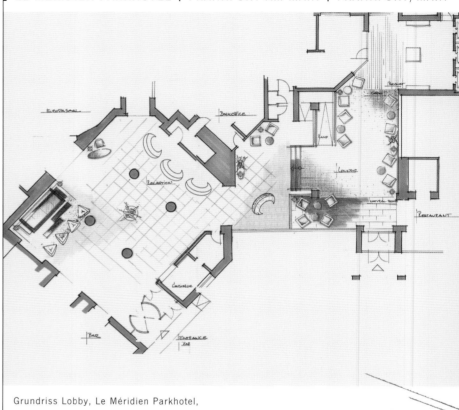

Floor plan of lobby,
Le Méridien Parkhotel,
Frankfurt/Main

Grundriss Lobby, Le Méridien Parkhotel,
Frankfurt am Main

CATEGORY | KATEGORIE
5*

THE BRIEF | AUFGABE
Complete refurbishment of public areas and rooms |
Komplettrenovierung Public Areas und Zimmer

SIZE | GRÖSSE
220 rooms | 220 Zimmer

HOTEL TYPE | HOTEL-TYP
City hotel | Stadthotel

PROJECT COMPLETED IN | BAUJAHR
2004-2009

COMPLETION PERIOD | BAUZEIT
In several phases | Phasenweise

AWARD | AUSZEICHNUNG
ADEX Award for Design Excellence 2009, Platinum

1

1 | The lobby: The three oval reception counters that face guests as they enter the lobby act as a welcoming counterpart to an otherwise austere interior.
2 | The white room: White pillars, white sofas and walls upholstered with light-colored leather create an atmosphere that invites guests to linger.

1 | Lobbyarbeit: Als lockeren Kontrast zur strengen, zentralen Halle empfangen den Gast drei ovale Rezeptionstresen an der Stirnseite.
2 | Viel Weißraum: Weiße Säulen, weiße Sofas und mit hellem Leder gepolsterte Wände laden den Gast zum Verweilen ein.

68_3

1

2

3

1 | Setting the mood: The light cream and brown tones of the walls contrast with the oak features.

2 | A shining example: The bronze-colored lamps cast a soft light on the dining area.

3 | Elegant dining: The "Le Parc" has been transformed into a contemporary restaurant. The mauve and beige tones match the restaurant's dark parquet and brown carpeting. The softly backlit alcoves are a perfect setting for decorative elements.

1 | Stimmungsmacher: Die Wände sind in hellem Crème bis hin zu hellem Braun gehalten und stehen im Kontrast zu dem Ausbauholz aus Eiche.

2 | Leuchtendes Beispiel: Bronzefarbene Leuchter tauchen den Essbereich in sanftes Licht.

3 | Schöner Speisen: Das Restaurant „Le Parc" wurde in ein modernes Restaurant verwandelt. Mauve und Beige korrespondieren mit dunklem Parkett und braunem Teppich. Blickfang sind die beleuchteten, in die Wand eingelassenen Zwischenräume, die Dekorationen Platz bieten.

1 | Bed chamber: Cream and brown tones combined with light blue accents and blue lighting dominate the visual design of the bedrooms.

2 | Clear picture: The television is mounted as a flat panel, thereby continuing the clear lines of the maplewood skirting.

3 | Furnishings: The brown floral design of the carpet matches the drapes and contributes to the warm, personal character of the hotel.

1 | Schlaf gemach: Crème- und Brauntöne kombiniert mit hellblau und blau leuchtenden Akzenten über dem Bettkopfteil sind vorherrschend in den Zimmern.

2 | Fern sehen: Der Fernseher wird als Paneel verwendet. Das helle Ahorn-Ausbauholz unterstützt dieses Konzept.

3 | Auslegeware: Der Teppich mit seinen großen braunen Blumen nimmt das Design der Vorhänge auf und unterstützt den warmen, persönlichen Charakter des Hotels.

CATEGORY | KATEGORIE
5*

THE BRIEF | AUFGABE
Design and realisation of a wellness
area | Einbau eines Wellnessbereiches

SIZE | GRÖSSE
650 m²

HOTEL TYPE | HOTEL-TYP
City hotel | Stadthotel

PROJECT COMPLETED IN | BAUJAHR
2004-2005

COMPLETION PERIOD | BAUZEIT
6 months | 6 Monate

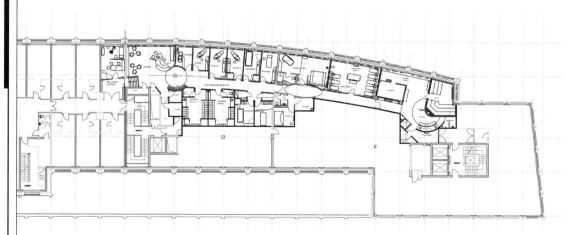

AUFGABE

In bester Hamburger Innenstadtlage bietet das Hotel Steigenberger mehr als 230 Zimmer und Luxussuiten mit höchstem Komfort. Bei der Umwandlung angrenzender Büroflächen in einen Day SPA sollte eine warme, wertige Atmosphäre geschaffen werden, die hanseatischen Chic zur Geltung bringt.

LÖSUNG

Nordisch by nature: Gezielt eingesetzte nordische Stilelemente unterstreichen die Lage des Objektes mit seiner Nähe zu den Fleeten und dem Hafen. Warmes Rot steht neben dunklem Holz und vermittelt ein einladendes, unaufgeregtes Ambiente. Zentral wichtig für das Konzept: Der freie Blick auf den Hafen und Hamburgs City.

THE BRIEF

Prominently located in Hamburg's inner city, Hotel Steigenberger offers its guests over 230 top-class rooms and luxury suites. Our task was to convert former office spaces into a day spa and create a warm, decorous atmosphere that underscores the hotel's Hanseatic chic.

THE SOLUTION

Nordic by nature: The studied application of Nordic style elements emphasises the hotel's unique location and its proximity to Hamburg's docklands and canals. The contrast of the spa's red and dark woods creates an inviting and tranquil atmosphere, while the superb view of Hamburg's docks afforded by the location forms a crucial element of the design concept.

THE RESULT

Hotel guests can work out or enjoy wellness, body therapy and beauty treatment in the spa's soothing ambience high above the rooftops of Hamburg.

ERGEBNIS

Hoch über den Dächern der Hansestadt genießt der Gast Fitness, Wellness, Body Therapy und Beautyanwendungen in harmonischem Ambiente.

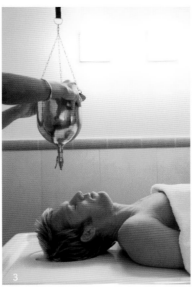

1 | Centered: The simple design of this rounded reception desk is typical of the entire Steigenberger Day Spa and emphasises the powerful visual aesthetics of the fine materials. The reception area features black granite, leather, wengé and warm red-jatobá parquet.

2 | Sweeping lines: The corridor leading to the various treatment rooms was designed according to feng shui principles – the elegant sweeping curve optically shortens the corridor.

3 | Oil change: Steigenberger Day Spa offers a range of luxurious and holistic Ayurvedic treatments.

1 | Im Zentrum: Der kreisförmige Empfangstresen ist wie alle Einbauten im Steigenberger Day SPA formal schlicht gehalten und wirkt durch seine edlen Materialien. Im Einsatz: schwarzer Granit, Leder, dunkles Wengeholz sowie rötliches Jatoba-Echtholzparkett.

2 | Schwungvoll: Der nach dem Feng Shui-Prinzip gestaltete Flur führt zu den verschiedenen Behandlungsräumen. Er folgt einem eleganten Schwung, der die Länge des Weges optisch aufhebt.

3 | Ölwechsel: Der ganzheitliche Ansatz des Ayurveda wird bei den Anwendungen im Steigenberger Day SPA Hamburg groß geschrieben.

STEIGENBERGER DAY SPA | HAMBURG

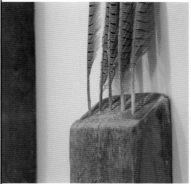

1

2

1 | A light breeze: Stylish decorative elements such as these seagull feathers exude Nordic lightness and maritime flair.
2 | Wellness programme: Guests can relax together in the elegant SPA Suite. Clear lines, transparent design and an intimate ambience define the room.

1 | Leichte Brise: Effektvolle Dekorationen wie Mövenfedern geben dem Raum das notwendige Maß an nordischer Leichtigkeit und Meeresfeeling.
2 | Verwöhnprogramm: Die elegante SPA-Suite lädt zum gemeinsamen Entspannen ein. Es dominieren klare Linien, viel Transparenz und ein wohnliches Ambiente.

STEIGENBERGER DAY SPA | HAMBURG

1

2

1 | Opaque: Guests enjoy a panoramic view of the docks from the sauna – the twigs and branches embedded within the glass protect guests from prying eyes.
2 | Panorama: The spa's rooftop fitness studio is a highlight in the truest sense of the word. The stunning views that guests enjoy from the studio's glass pavilion and balcony more than compensate them for their exertions.

1 | Blickdicht: Auch aus der Sauna kann man auf das Geschehen am Hafen schauen. Einen zuverlässigen Blickschutz stellt das in die Glasscheiben integrierte Geäst dar.
2 | Blickpunkt Hamburg: Ein buchstäbliches Highlight ist der Fitnessbereich auf dem Dach des Hotels. Der Glaspavillon mit Terrasse gewährt beim Training einen Rundumblick und entschädigt für manchen vergossenen Schweißtropfen.

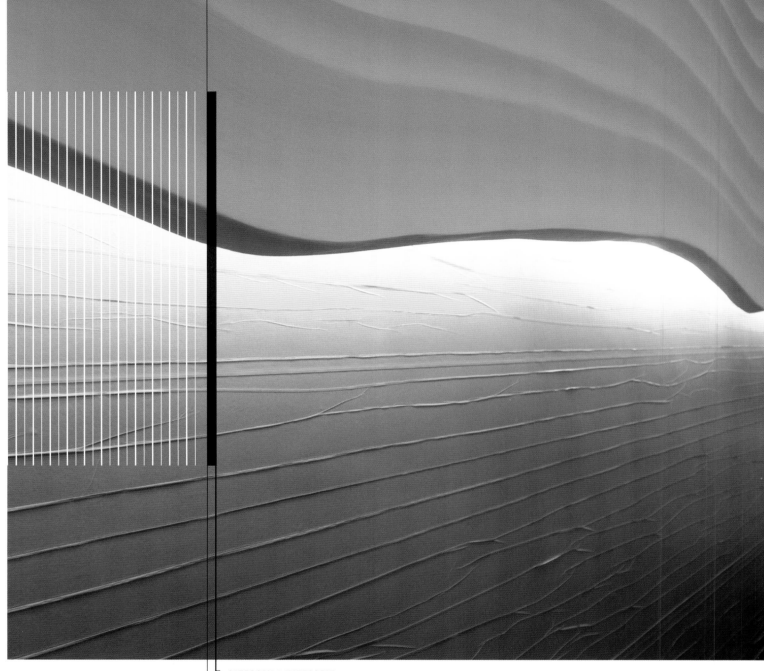

CATEGORY | KATEGORIE
Fine dining restaurant in 5* hotel | Gourmetrestaurant in 5* Hotel

THE BRIEF | AUFGABE
Complete refurbishment of restaurant with installation of a new buffet section |
Komplettrenovierung des Restaurants mit Einbau neuer Buffetanlage

SIZE | GRÖSSE
520 m²

HOTEL TYPE | HOTEL-TYP
City hotel | Stadthotel

PROJECT COMPLETED IN | BAUJAHR
2009

COMPLETION PERIOD | BAUZEIT
2 months | 2 Monate

THE BRIEF

The "Calla" Restaurant in Hamburg's Steigenberger Hotel is renowned for its outstanding cuisine. But the restaurant's original design had outlived its time and a new concept was needed: Bright, friendly, open, and with a clear floor plan to facilitate spatial orientation.

THE CONCEPT

The perfect wave: The restaurant's close proximity to the docks was a key consideration for the new design concept. Abstract wave forms decorating the floor coverings and wall-mounted handmade stucco reliefs reflect this theme. The buffet and walls follow an organic design principle, forming a stimulating contrast to the straight lines of the building's Hanseatic architecture.

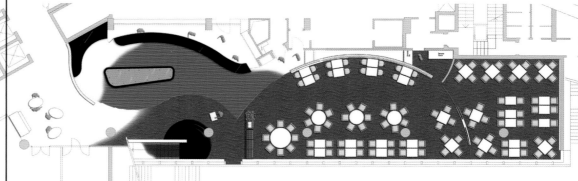

AUFGABE

Das Restaurant „Calla" im Hamburger Steigenberger Hotel ist bekannt für seine hervorragende Küche. Doch der vorherige Look passte nicht mehr. Alles sollte heller, freundlicher und offener werden, klarer strukturiert, um dem Gast eine Orientierung zu bieten.

KONZEPT

Die perfekte Welle: Die Nähe zum Fleet spielt eine entscheidende Rolle bei dem Konzept. Abstrahierte Wellenformen zieren den Teppich, handgearbeitete Stuckreliefs an den Wänden nehmen die Wellenform auf. Auch die Buffets und Wände folgen diesem organischen Gestaltungsprinzip und bilden einen spannungsreichen Kontrast zu der geradlinigen hanseatischen Architektur des restlichen Gebäudes.

Tone-in-tone: None of the colors dominates. Instead, soft cream tones are combined with darker, earthier tones.

Ton in Ton: Keine Farbe dominiert. Stattdessen: sanfte Crèmetöne in Kombination mit dunkleren, erdigen Farben.

RESTAURANT „CALLA", STEIGENBERGER HOTEL | HAMBURG

1 | Shining brightly: The mood of the room can be altered with the fully dimmable lighting system.
2 | Open to new ideas: Dishes are prepared individually at the new buffet zone's open demonstration kitchen.

1 | Heller Schein: Mit Hilfe eines komplett dimmbaren Lichtsystems lässt sich die Stimmung der Tageszeit anpassen.
2 | Offen für Neues: In der offenen Show-küche innerhalb der neuen Buffetanlage werden Speisen individuell zubereitet.

Mercur

THE BRIEF

Think global, build local. We were commissioned to create an individual design concept to reposition 15 Novotel into Mercure hotels. The designs were to emphasise regional character, without resorting to clichés.

AUFGABE

Think global, build local: Für die Repositionierung von 15 Novotels zu Mercure Hotels sollte ein individuelles Gestaltungskonzept für jedes Haus entwickelt werden. Die Vorgabe: Die regionalen Besonderheiten hervorheben, ohne Klischees zu bedienen.

THE SOLUTION

The power of images: the designs
draw on iconic features of the
respective locations. The interior
designers worked closely with
photographers during the planning
phase of each project.

LÖSUNG

Die Kraft der Bilder:
Die Besonderheiten
der jeweiligen Stadt
flossen in die Ent-
würfe mit ein. Bereits
während der Planung
gab es dabei eine
enge Zusammenarbeit
zwischen Fotografen
und Innenarchitekten.

1

CATEGORY | KATEGORIE
3* superior

THE BRIEF | AUFGABE
Complete refurbishment of public areas and rooms |
Komplettrenovierung Public Areas und Zimmer

SIZE | GRÖSSE
186 rooms | 186 Zimmer

HOTEL TYPE | HOTEL-TYP
Business/city hotel | Businesshotel/Stadthotel

PROJECT COMPLETED IN | BAUJAHR
2005

COMPLETION PERIOD | BAUZEIT
3 months | 3 Monate

1 | Centerpoint: The bar
is the hub of the hotel.
2 | Air show: Large
aerodynamic forms are
reminiscent of the wings
of early aircraft.
3 | A quiet haven: The
lobby with fireplace and
reading corner.

1 | Mittelpunkt: Die Bar
als Zentrum des Hotels.
2 | Flugschau: Große,
aerodynamische Formen
erinnern an die Tragflächen
erster Flugzeuge.
3 | Rückzugsort: Die Lobby
mit Kamin und Leseecke.

2

3

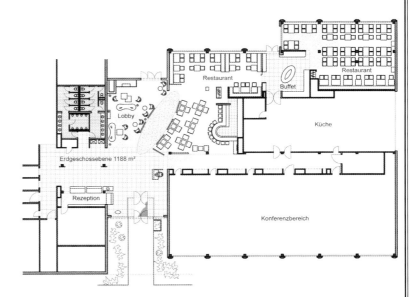

Restaurant

Restaurant

Buffet

Küche

Lobby

Erdgeschossebene 1188 m²

Rezeption

Konferenzbereich

CATEGORY | KATEGORIE
3* superior

THE BRIEF | AUFGABE
Complete refurbishment of public areas and rooms |
Komplettrenovierung Public Areas und Zimmer

SIZE | GRÖSSE
119 rooms | 119 Zimmer

HOTEL TYPE | HOTEL-TYP
Business/city hotel | Businesshotel/Stadthotel

PROJECT COMPLETED IN | BAUJAHR
2005

COMPLETION PERIOD | BAUZEIT
3 months | 3 Monate

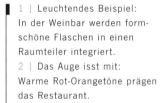

1 | Leuchtendes Beispiel:
In der Weinbar werden form-
schöne Flaschen in einen
Raumteiler integriert.
2 | Das Auge isst mit:
Warme Rot-Orangetöne prägen
das Restaurant.

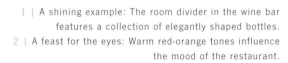

1 | A shining example: The room divider in the wine bar
features a collection of elegantly shaped bottles.
2 | A feast for the eyes: Warm red-orange tones influence
the mood of the restaurant.

MERCURE HOTEL | BERLIN CITY WEST

1   2

CATEGORY | KATEGORIE
4* superior

THE BRIEF | AUFGABE
Complete refurbishment of public areas and rooms |
Komplettrenovierung Public Areas und Zimmer

SIZE | GRÖSSE
112 rooms | 112 Zimmer

HOTEL TYPE | HOTEL-TYP
Business/city hotel | Businesshotel/Stadthotel

PROJECT COMPLETED IN | BAUJAHR
2005

COMPLETION PERIOD | BAUZEIT
3 months | 3 Monate

93_3

1+2 | Artistic inspiration: This armchair and sofa are reminiscent of Niki de Saint Phalle's famous Nana figures. The French painter and sculptor had a special relationship with the city of Hanover.

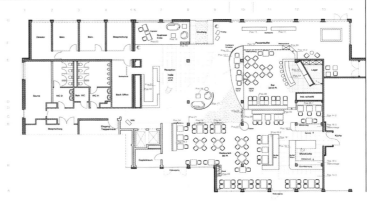

1+2 | Die Nanas standen Pate: Die Sitzgarnitur erinnert an die berühmten Figuren der französischen Künstlerin Niki de Saint Phalle. Warum? Die Malerin und Bildhauerin hatte eine besondere Beziehung zu Hannover.

CATEGORY | KATEGORIE
4*

THE BRIEF | AUFGABE
Complete refurbishment of public areas
and rooms | Komplettrenovierung Public
Areas und Zimmer

SIZE | GRÖSSE
245 rooms | 245 Zimmer

HOTEL TYPE | HOTEL-TYP
Business/city hotel | Businesshotel/
Stadthotel

PROJECT COMPLETED IN | BAUJAHR
2005

COMPLETION PERIOD | BAUZEIT
4 months | 4 Monate

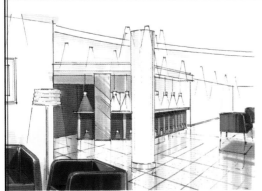

City of beer:
This dining area
features striking
beer-themed
panels.

Bier her:
In München ist
das Bier nicht nur
in den Gläsern,
sondern auch an
der Wand.

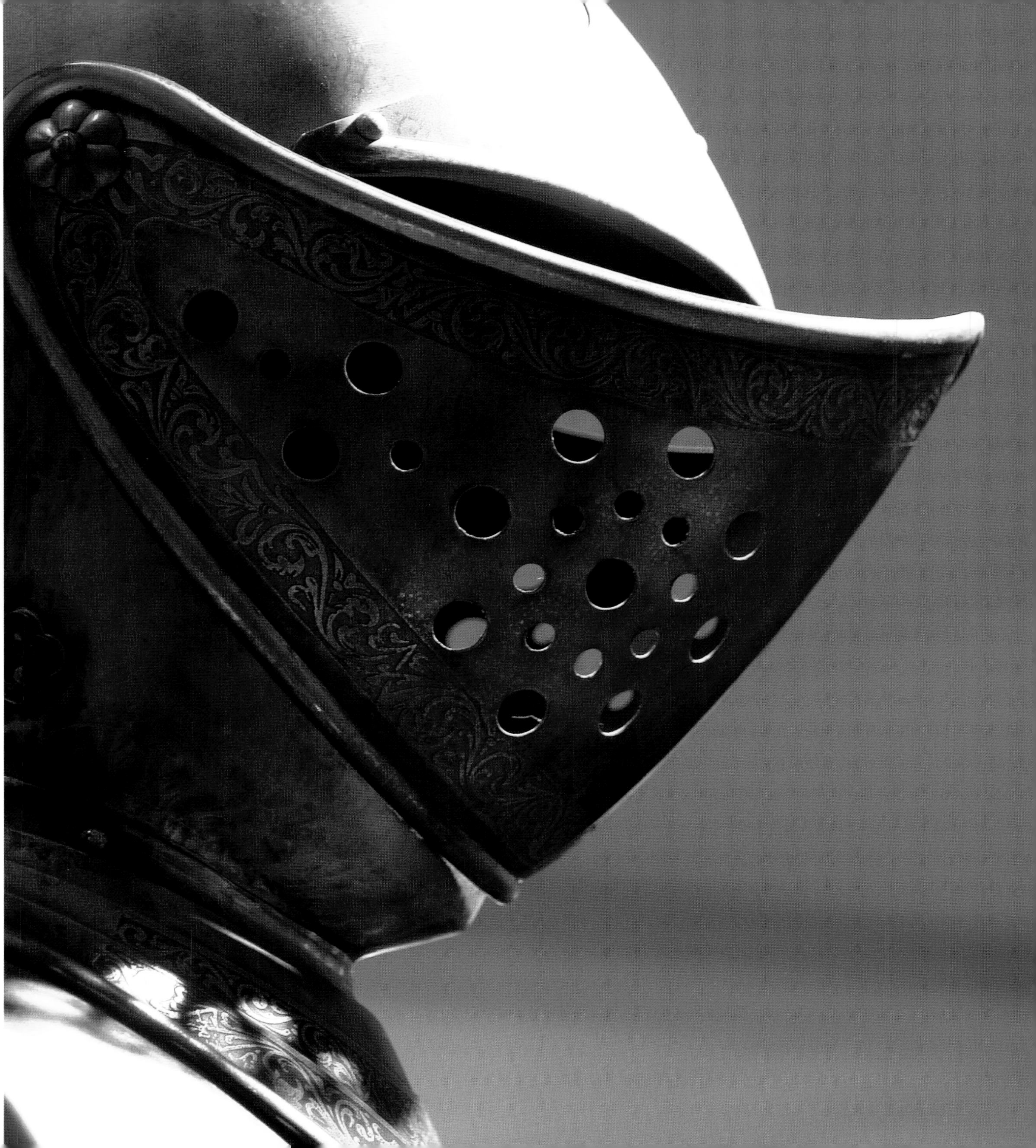

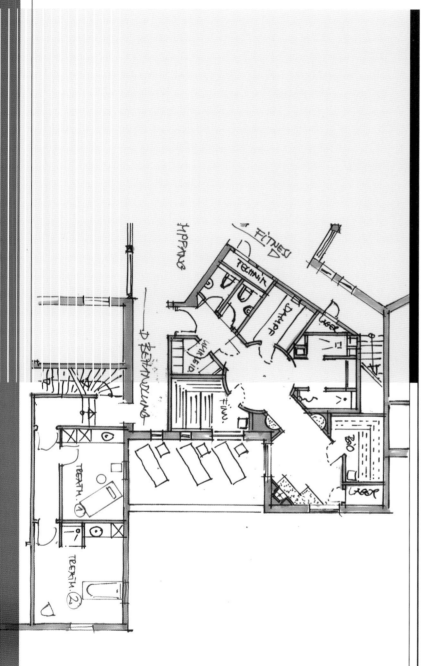

HOTEL RITTER | DURBACH

CATEGORY | KATEGORIECATEGORY
4* superior

THE BRIEF | AUFGABE
Complete refurbishment of public areas
and rooms | Komplettrenovierung Public
Areas und Zimmer

SIZE | GRÖSSE
60 rooms | 60 Zimmer

HOTEL TYPE | HOTEL-TYP
Design and wellness hotel | Design-
und Wellnesshotel

PROJECT COMPLETED IN | BAUJAHR
2008

COMPLETION PERIOD | BAUZEIT
8 months | 8 Monate

THE BRIEF

Situated on the idyllic Baden Wine Route
between Alsace and the Black Forest,
Hotel Ritter in Durbach has a history
that stretches back 500 years. We were
commissioned to transform it into a
four-star superior design hotel. The
challenge: To breathe new life into the
hotel while preserving its
traditional flair.

THE SOLUTION

Welcome to Durbach: A new era begins
in this small southern German town.
The white cuckoo clocks tell international time. The hotel's distinctive
curios and objects d'art were dusted off
and infused with modern panache.
The new colors and materials are
refreshing and never seem pretentious.

AUFGABE

Das Traditions-Hotel Ritter in Durbach, idyllisch an der badischen
Weinstraße zwischen Elsass und Schwarzwald gelegen, verfügt
über eine 500 Jahre alte Geschichte. Der Auftrag: Die Umge-
staltung des Hotels in ein 4-Sterne Superior Designhotel.
Die Herausforderung: Die Tradition des Hauses bewahren und
mit neuen Akzenten beleben.

LÖSUNG

Welcome to Durbach: Eine neue Zeit hält Einzug in der kleinen
süddeutschen Stadt. Weiße Kuckucksuhren zeigen internationale
Zeiten an. Typische Gegenstände aus der Region werden
modern eingesetzt, alte Requisiten aufpoliert. Neue Farben und
Materialien wirken in den alten Mauern erfrischend, aber nie
aufgesetzt.

100_3

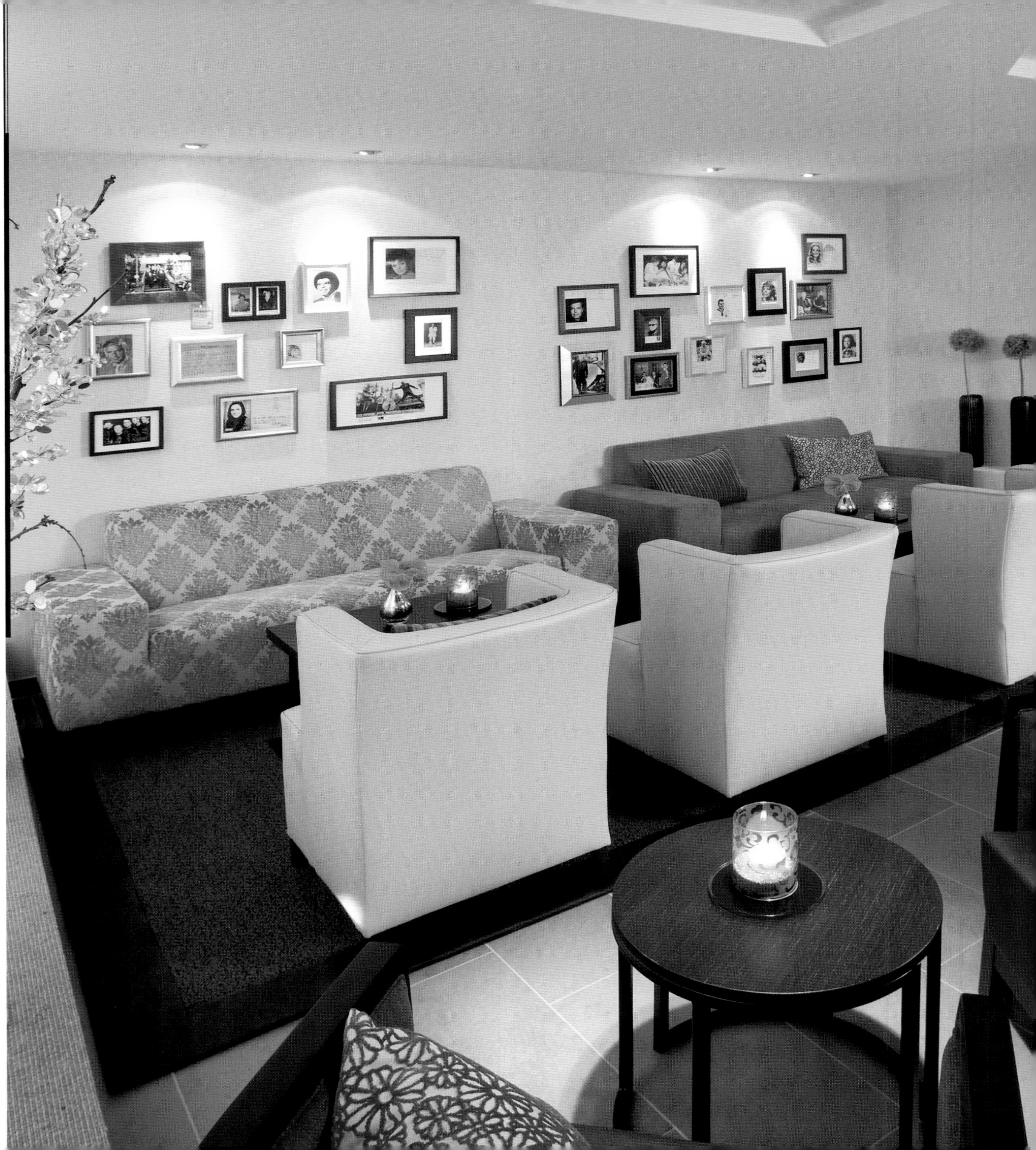

1 | Hall of Fame: This photo gallery features some of Hotel Ritter's more illustrious guests, including former German Chancellor Helmut Kohl, Carl Friedrich von Weizsäcker, the Dalai Lama and numerous actors and actresses.

2 | New York, Durbach, Tokyo: The hotel's new spirit is reflected in the design of the reception area. The cuckoo clocks mounted on the fuchsia-colored wall are a real highlight and display the time in Durbach, London, New York, Hong Kong and Tokyo.

1 | Hall of Fame: Die Fotogalerie zeigt illustre Gäste des Hotel Ritter. Darunter der ehemalige Bundeskanzler Helmut Kohl, Carl Friedrich von Weizsäcker, der Dalai Lama sowie viele berühmte Schauspieler.

2 | In New York, Durbach, Tokio: Der neue Geist des Hotels spiegelt sich auch beim Empfang wider: Highlight sind hier die Kuckucksuhren an der Fuchsia farbenen Wand. Sie zeigen neben der Uhrzeit in Durbach auch die von London, New York, Honkong und Tokio an.

HOTEL RITTER | DURBACH

1 | Room art: The bedrooms are a blend of traditional and modern designs featuring a range of fabric patterns and apple-wood veneer.

2 | Sleep like a king: The stylized four-poster bed is a nod to the hotel's medieval origins.

1 | Raum Kunst: In den Zimmern setzt sich der Mix aus Tradition und Moderne fort: Eingestreute Stoffmotive und die starken Furnierbilder des Apfelholzes kommen auch wieder zur Geltung.

2 | Ritterlich schlafen: Das Thema Himmelbett darf in einem Hotel mit dem Namen Ritter nicht fehlen.

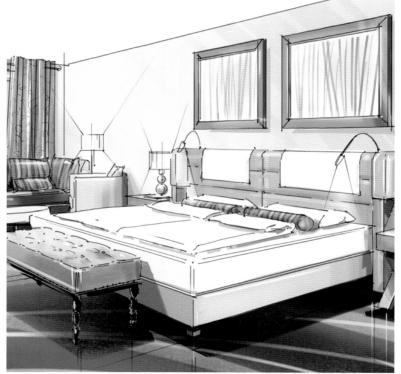

| | | | | | | | | | | | | | | | | | | | | | | |

Rest in peace: The color composition evokes an atmosphere of tranquillity. The colors, which range from cream and sand tones through to grey, reflect the region's landscape.

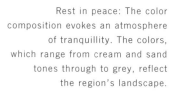

Ruhe sanft: Die gesamte Farbwelt lässt das Auge ruhen – alles ist in Crème-, Sand- bis Grautönen gehalten und spiegelt die Natur der Region wider.

Live gastronomy: Guests to the hotel can watch the restaurant chefs from their seats at the "kitchen table". The rustic ambience of the adjoining dining room is guaranteed to help guests work up an appetite.

Küchenschlacht live: Gäste können vom „Küchentisch" aus den Köchen bei der Arbeit zusehen. Der angrenzende Speiseraum mit seinem rustikalen Ambiente macht schon bildhaft Appetit auf mehr.

Bambi reloaded: In einem
Séparée des Restaurants
empfangen eine Reihe Geweihe
den Gast.

Bambi reloaded: Antlers
adorn the walls of one of the
restaurant's private rooms.

The blue hour: The newly extended spa area covers 600 square meters and features a swimming pool, saunas, a fitness studio and several relaxation areas.

Blaue Stunde: Der SPA-Bereich wurde auf über 600 m² erweitert und bietet neben dem Pool, Saunen und einem Fitnessraum viele Ruhezonen an.

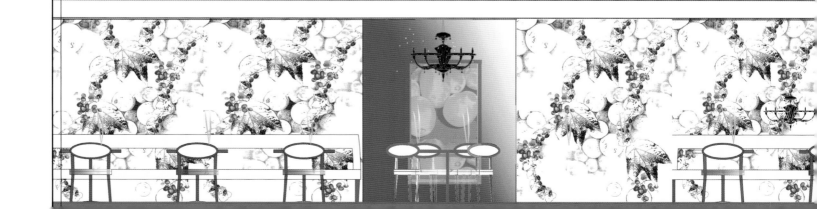

Weinselig: Für das Gourmetrestaurant „Wilder Ritter"
wurde eine Tapete gestaltet, die
das Thema Wein in den Mittelpunkt stellt. Eine Referenz
an die Gegend.

In vino veritas:
The wallpaper was
designed exclusively
for the hotel's
fine dining restaurant
"Wilder Ritter" and
pays homage to the
region's viticultural
traditions.

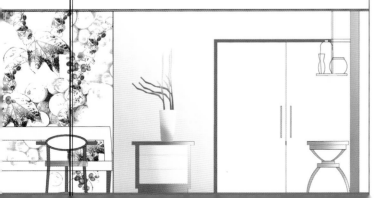

1

1 | In paradise: The spacious
dining table located in the wine cellar
seats up to twelve persons.
2 | Underground: The vaulted cellar's
authentic atmosphere was preserved – a
clear-cut case of less being more.
3 | The knights' parlour: Some
things simply cannot be improved on.
The Ritterstube specialises in rustic
culinary delights.

1 | Im Paradies: Die große Tafel
im begehbaren Weinkeller bietet
Platz für 12 Personen.
2 | Unter Tage: Die authentische
Atmosphäre im Gewölbekeller
wurde erhalten. Weniger ist
hier mehr.
3 | Ritterstube: Es gibt Dinge,
die kann man nicht verbessern.
In der Ritterstube wird die boden-
ständige Küche gepflegt.

HOTEL RITTER | DURBACH

2   3

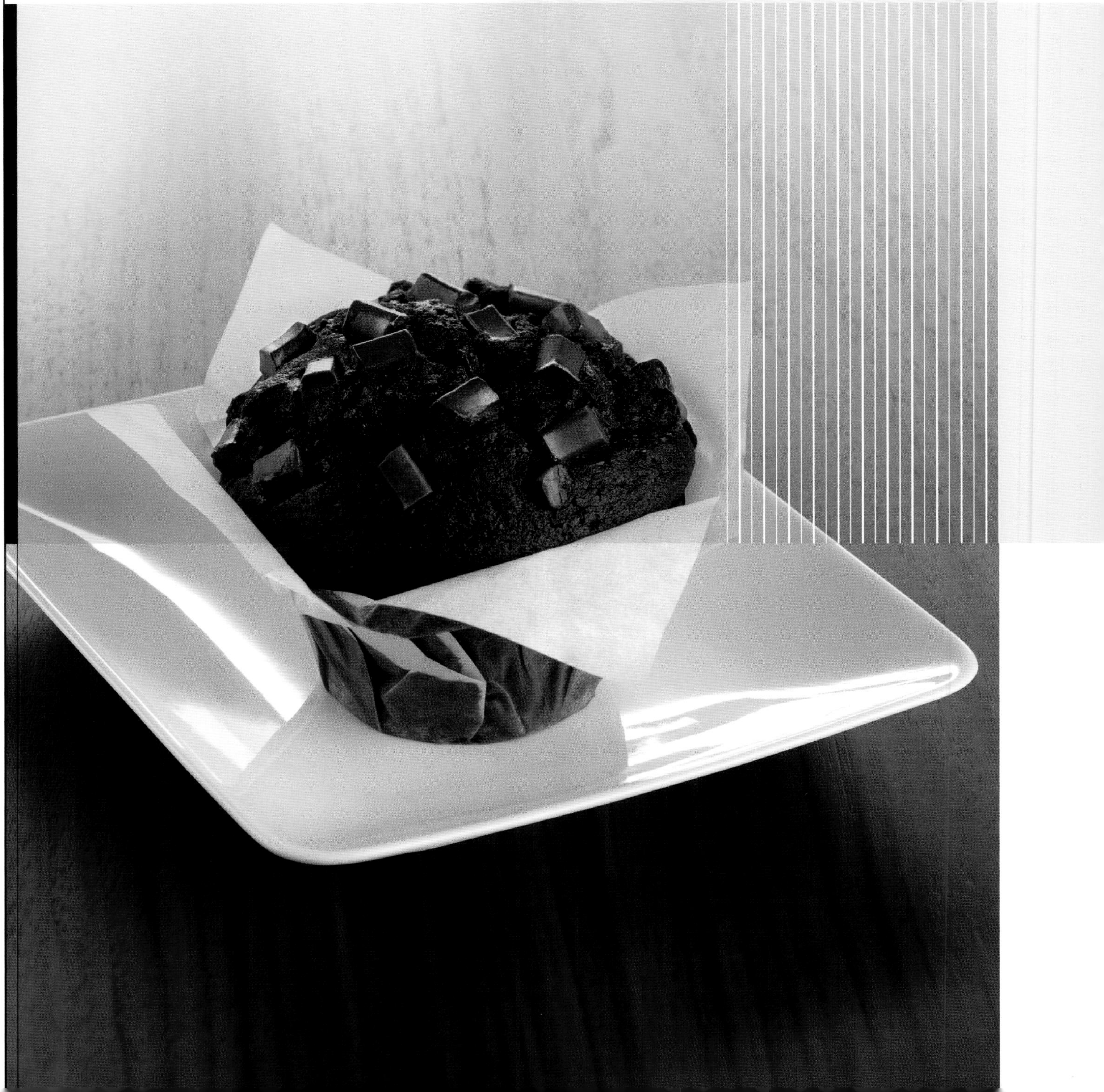

THE BRIEF

Our client wanted to lose its burger-
and-fries image in favor of a more
stylish coffee shop flair. The task was
to develop a café design concept that
would help McDonald's retain its
younger customer segment.

THE SOLUTION

Two different concepts were developed
that could be adapted to the design
of individual restaurants, and matched
to specific locations and customer
expectations: "Club 54" and "Sydney".

AUFGABE

Weg vom Burger-Image hin zum
schicken Coffee-Shop. Für McDonald's
sollte ein Café-Konzept entwickelt
werden, das junge Kundengruppen
wieder zurück bringt zu McDonald's.

LÖSUNG

Entwicklung von zwei unterschied-
lichen Konzepten, die sich mit den
Designs in den Restaurants kombi-
nieren lassen und auf verschiedene
Standorte und Kundenerwartungen
eingehen: „Club 54" und „Sydney".

REALISATION

The "Club 54" design features a young, fresh style and employs powerful color accents to attract customers. The "Sydney" concept has a more classical feel, which is underscored by the sober black leather armchairs, and the warm red and golden-yellow hues.

THE RESULT

Customers reacted positively to both concepts, leading to significant increases in revenues in the refurbished restaurants. The "Sydney" and "Club 54" design concepts have since been replicated approximately 500 times in Germany, enabling McDonald's McCafé brand to become the market leader for the German café sector in just four years.

UMSETZUNG

Das Konzept „Club 54" verkörpert einen jungen, frischen Stil, der den Gast durch farbig knackige Akzente hereinlockt. Das Konzept „Sydney" hat eine klassischere Ausrichtung, die unterstrichen wird durch die Kombination mit strengen schwarzen Ledersesseln, warmen Rottönen und Goldgelb.

ERGEBNIS

Beide Gestaltungskonzepte wurden von Kunden hervorragend angenommen und lassen die Umsätze der umgebauten Restaurants deutlich ansteigen. Inzwischen wurden die Konzepte „Sydney" und „Club 54" in Deutschland ca. 500 mal realisiert. Innerhalb von vier Jahren gelang es McDonald's, jenseits des schnellen Burgers mit seinen McCafés Marktführer für den Bereich Cafés in Deutschland zu werden.

1

2

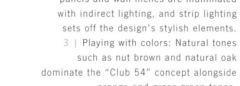

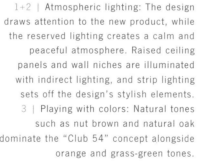

3

1+2 | Atmospheric lighting: The design draws attention to the new product, while the reserved lighting creates a calm and peaceful atmosphere. Raised ceiling panels and wall niches are illuminated with indirect lighting, and strip lighting sets off the design's stylish elements.
3 | Playing with colors: Natural tones such as nut brown and natural oak dominate the "Club 54" concept alongside orange and grass-green tones.

1+2 | Stimmungslichter: Die neuen Konzepte sollten effektvoll auf das neue Produkt hinweisen aber mit gedämpftem Licht gleichzeitig eine ruhige Atmosphäre widerspiegeln. So werden beispielsweise erhöhte Deckenfelder oder Wandnischen mit indirektem Licht angestrahlt, und Streiflichter setzen Raumelemente sanft in Szene.
3 | Farbspiel: Beim Konzept „Club 54" werden Naturtöne wie Nussbaum und Eiche natur mit Orange- und Grasgrünfarbtönen gemixt.

CATEGORY | KATEGORIE
Fast food

THE BRIEF | AUFGABE
Renovation and installation of McCafé | Renovierung mit Einbau McCafé

SIZE | GRÖSSE
35 m²

RESTAURANT TYPE | RESTAURANT-TYP
Fast-food restaurant and McCafé – "Club 54" design concept | Schnellrestaurant mit McCafé-Konzept „Club 54"

PROJECT COMPLETED IN | BAUJAHR
2006

COMPLETION PERIOD | BAUZEIT
2 weeks | 2 Wochen

FRANCHISE HOLDER | FRANCHISENEHMER
Burkhard Timme

Striking: The milk coffee color and giant logo on the ceiling give the "Sydney" design concept a highly visible profile.

Plakativ: Beim Gestaltungs-konzept „Sydney" weist ein warmer Milchkaffeefarbton an der Decke mit einem riesigen Schriftzug schon von weitem auf die neue Location hin.

McCAFÉ | DIBBERSEN

CATEGORY | KATEGORIE
Fast food

THE BRIEF | AUFGABE
Renovation and installation of McCafé |
Renovierung mit Einbau McCafé

SIZE | GRÖSSE
43 m²

RESTAURANT TYPE | RESTAURANT-TYP
Fast-food restaurant and McCafé –
"Sydney" design concept | Schnellres-
taurant mit McCafé-Konzept „Sydney"

PROJECT COMPLETED IN | BAUJAHR
2007

COMPLETION PERIOD | BAUZEIT
2 weeks | 2 Wochen

**FRANCHISE HOLDER | FRANCHISE-
NEHMER**
Frauke Petersen-Hanson

Color and form at play: The
"Club 54" concept includes stunning
ceiling features, rounded furniture
and eye-catching wall niches.

Farb- und Formenspiel: Beim
Konzept „Club 54" ergänzen sich
kreisrunde Formen in Decke und
Mobiliar mit in die Wand einge-
lassenen Streifenmotiven.

CATEGORY | KATEGORIE
Fast food

THE BRIEF | AUFGABE
Renovation and installation of McCafé | Renovierung mit Einbau
McCafé

SIZE | GRÖSSE
52 m²

RESTAURANT TYPE | RESTAURANT-TYP
Fast-food restaurant and McCafé – "Club 54" design concept |
Schnellrestaurant mit McCafé-Konzept „Club 54"

PROJECT COMPLETED IN | BAUJAHR
2006

COMPLETION PERIOD | BAUZEIT
2 weeks | 2 Wochen

FRANCHISE HOLDER | FRANCHISENEHMER
Kurt Neubaumer

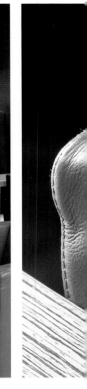

CATEGORY | KATEGORIE
Fast food

THE BRIEF | AUFGABE
Renovation and installation of McCafé |
Renovierung mit Einbau McCafé

SIZE | GRÖSSE
63 m²

RESTAURANT TYPE | RESTAURANT-TYP
Fast-food restaurant and McCafé – "Sydney" design concept |
Schnellrestaurant mit McCafé-Konzept „Sydney"

PROJECT COMPLETED IN | BAUJAHR
2007

COMPLETION PERIOD | BAUZEIT
2 weeks | 2 Wochen

FRANCHISE HOLDER | FRANCHISENEHMER
Christian Eckstein

McCAFÉ | OSNABRÜCK

Lounge schön: Beide Konzepte
bieten mit Loungebereichen aus
kleinen Sesseln und Poufs einen Ort
zum Verweilen an und setzen sich
bei den Shop-in-Shop-Lösungen vom
übrigen Restaurant ab.

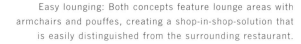

Easy lounging: Both concepts feature lounge areas with
armchairs and pouffes, creating a shop-in-shop-solution that
is easily distinguished from the surrounding restaurant.

CATEGORY | KATEGORIE
4 – 5*

THE BRIEF | AUFGABE
Creation of a themed island stand |
Realisierung einer Themeninsel

SIZE | GRÖSSE
500 m²

TYPE | TYP
Trade fair stand | Messestand

PROJECT COMPLETED IN | BAUJAHR
2008

COMPLETION PERIOD | BAUZEIT
3 days | 3 Tage

THE BRIEF

Hogatec 2008: The task was to present a range of concepts for hotel rooms at the special show "Ambience and Ambitions". The presentation was to showcase unusual design ideas and innovative concepts for the hospitality industry.

THE CONCEPT

The trade fair stand was opened with the motto "Hospitality – Tradition meets Modern Design" and featured 500 square meters of inspiring contemporary room design and also traditional variations for five-star hotels. A timeline through the exhibition area illustrated the history of the hospitality industry.

AUFGABE

Hogatec 2008: Im Rahmen der Sonderschau „Ambiente und Ambitionen" sollten verschiedene Hotelzimmerkonzepte präsentiert werden. Ziel des Themenstandes war es, die Hotellerie auf ungewöhnliche Designideen aufmerksam zu machen und neue Wege der Gestaltung zu eröffnen.

KONZEPT

Unter dem Thema „Hotellerie zwischen Tradition und Moderne" wurden auf 500 m² inspirierende, zeitgenössische Designs und traditionellere Varianten für Hotelzimmer der 5-Sterne-Kategorie gezeigt. Die Ausstellungsfläche wurde getrennt durch eine Zeitachse; sie vermittelte dem Besucher die Geschichte der Hotellerie.

Grünfläche: Nachhaltigkeit und ökologisches Bewusstsein stehen bei diesem Entwurf im Vordergrund. Das Ergebnis ist ein verspielter, märchenhafter Entwurf, der sich mit Witz dem Anspruch „Green" widmet und die Möglichkeiten aufzeigt, Ökodesign im Hotelbusiness zu realisieren.

Green space: "Sustainability" and "eco-awareness" are the watchwords here. The playful design takes a smart, upbeat approach to "green" values and demonstrates how eco-design can be successfully implemented in the hotel business.

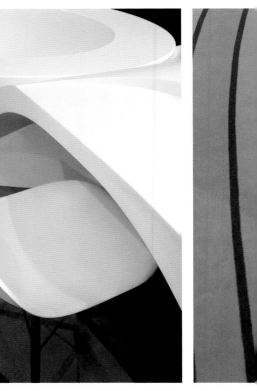

1

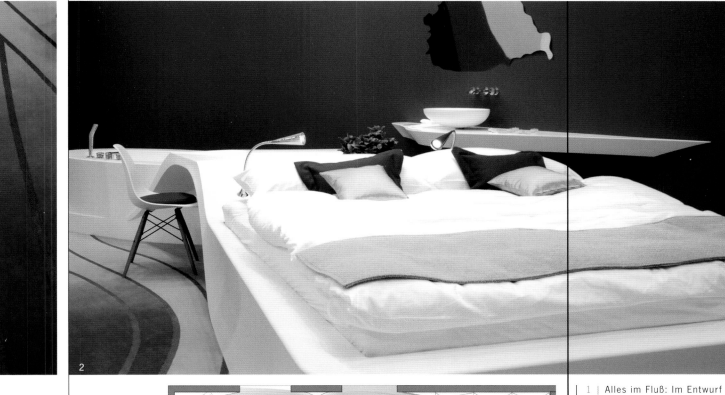

2

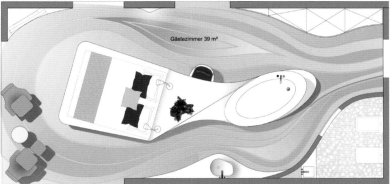

Gästezimmer 39 m²

1 | Alles im Fluß: Im Entwurf „organic trace" umspielen extrem organische Formen die „Wellness-insel" im Raum.

2 | Alleskönner: Die weiße Skulptur im Zentrum des Raumes vereint die Funktionen von Bett, Schreibtisch und Badewanne.

1 | It's all about the flow: A "wellness island" nestles among organic forms in the "organic trace" design concept.

2 | Versatility: The white sculpture in the center of the room is a bath, desk and bed all in one.

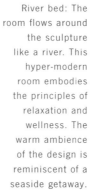

River bed: The room flows around the sculpture like a river. This hyper-modern room embodies the principles of relaxation and wellness. The warm ambience of the design is reminiscent of a seaside getaway.

Flussbett: Die Skulptur wird wie ein Stein im Flussbett umspült. Dieser hypermoderne Raum symbolisiert „Relaxen und Wohlfühlen" und vermittelt eine Wohnlichkeit, die an ein Haus am Meer erinnert.

▌HOGATEC 2008 | DÜSSELDORF

New objectivity:
Luminosity, clear
lines and a
pleasantly cool
design distinguish
this hotel room.

Neue Sachlichkeit:
Ein Hotelzimmer mit heller
Leichtigkeit, klaren Formen und
angenehmer Kühle.

The sign of the flower: This design plays with classical design elements, combining contemporary and historical styles such as Art Deco.

Im Zeichen der Blume: Dieser Entwurf spielt bewusst mit klassischen Stilelementen, wobei aktuelle und historische Formen wie Art Deco u.a. miteinander kombiniert werden.

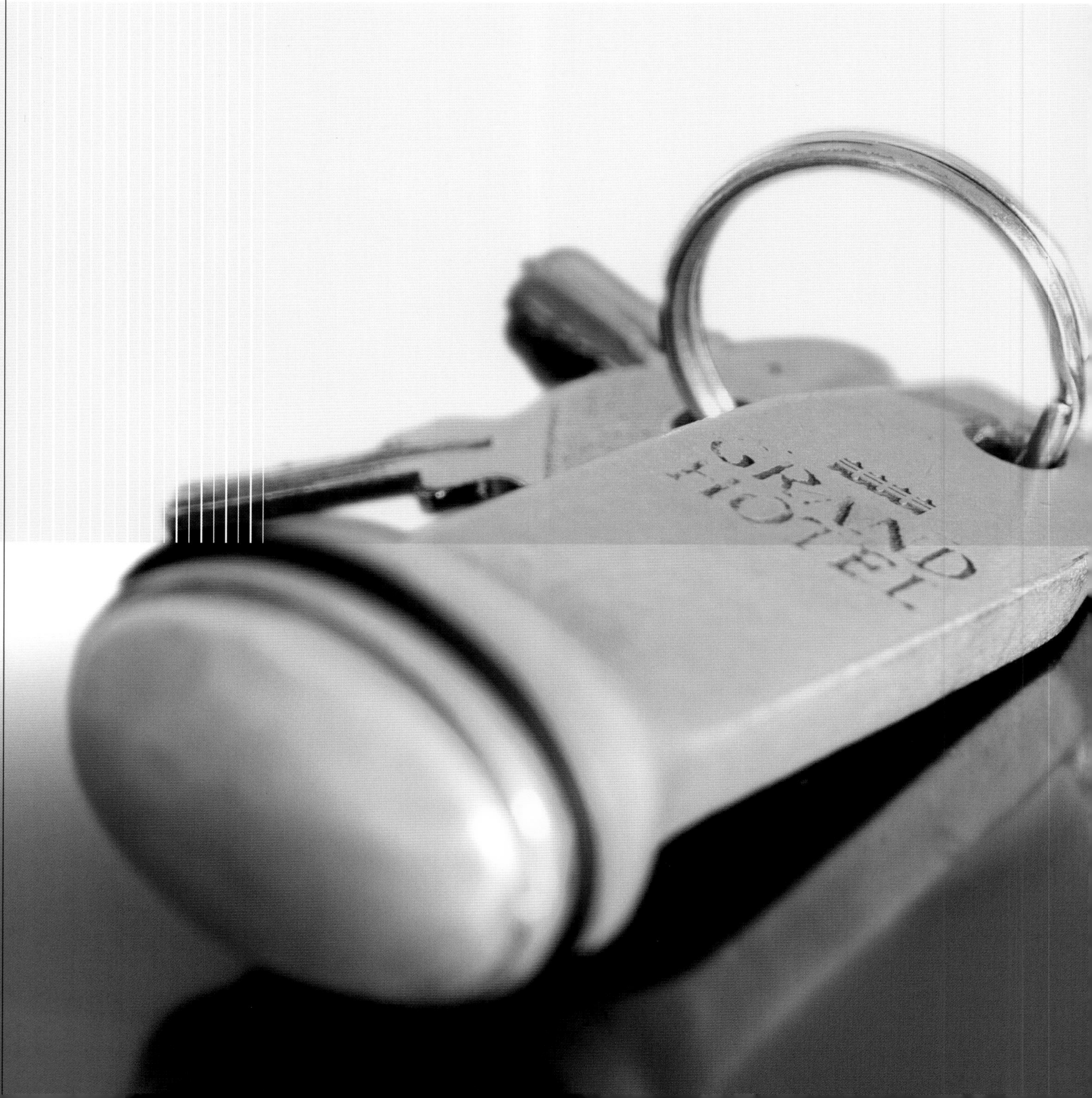
GRAND
HOTEL

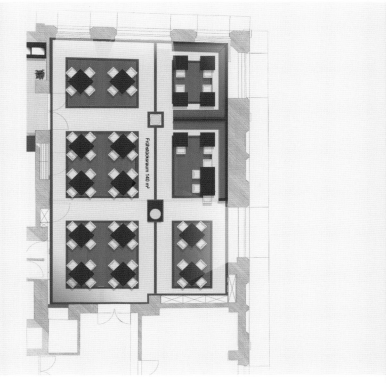

CATEGORY | KATEGORIE
5*

THE BRIEF | AUFGABE
Renovation of restaurant and rooms |
Komplettrenovierung Restaurant und
Zimmer

SIZE | GRÖSSE
186 rooms | 186 Zimmer

HOTEL TYPE | HOTEL-TYP
City hotel | Stadthotel

**PROJECT COMPLETED IN |
BAUJAHR**
2008-2009

COMPLETION PERIOD | BAUZEIT
2009

THE BRIEF

Le Méridien Grand Hotel
Nuremberg is surrounded by
history. Nuremberg was the
birthplace of Albrecht Dürer and
the golden city of the German
Renaissance. The challenge: To
renovate and refurbish the hotel's
186 rooms, while preserving their
marble Jugendstil bathrooms.
Plus: to design a dual-purpose
restaurant with buffet that can
double as a conference room
if necessary.

THE SOLUTION

The design concept is based
on classical European styles.
The forms, colors and details of
the design offer contemporary
interpretations of
traditional elements.

AUFGABE

Das Le Méridien Grand Hotel Nürnberg ist von Geschichte
umringt. Nürnberg war die Heimat von Albrecht Dürer und
die goldene Stadt der deutschen Renaissance. Die Anforderungen: Umbau und Renovierung von 186 Zimmern, deren
Jugendstil-Marmorbäder erhalten bleiben sollten. Zudem:
Gestaltung eines Restaurants mit Buffetbereich, das auch
als Konferenzbereich genutzt werden kann.

LÖSUNG

Die traditionelle europäische Klassik steht im Mittelpunkt
des gesamten Konzeptes. Formen, Farben und Details der
Entwürfe erinnern an Bekanntes, sind aber neu interpretiert.

142_3

143_3

1 | Dining in style: Black and white, complimented by warmer tones, dominate the Fürstenhof restaurant's visual design. Stylish black wall-mounted mouldings frame the wallpaper's silver floral design.

2 | Sophisticated stripes: With its pinstriped floor coverings and reserved style, this dual-purpose room can also be used for conference events.

1 | Schöner speisen: Die dominierenden Farben im Restaurant Fürstenhof sind Schwarz-Weiß, gemischt mit warmen Tönen. Das silberne Blumendekor der Tapete wurde gerahmt mit schwarzen Setzleisten auf der Wand.

2 | Edler Streifen: Der Teppich zeigt sich im edlen Nadelstreif. Durch das zurückhaltende Design kann der Raum auch für Konferenzen genutzt werden.

1 | Soundproof: Sweet dreams under a lavishly quilted headboard.
2 | European chic: This sofa in a classic hound's-tooth pattern plays on Chanel designs. The tables and bedside cabinets conjure up memories of an era when people still travelled with plenty of luggage.

1 | Schallschlucker: Aufwändiges Steppwerk am Bettkopf versüßt die Träume.
2 | European chic: Das Sofa im klassischen Hahnentrittmuster spielt mit Entwürfen von Chanel. Tische und Nachttische erinnern an die Zeit, als die Herrschaft noch mit großem Gepäck anreiste.

LE MERIDIEN GRAND HOTEL | NUREMBERG | NÜRNBERG

1 | Black and white: The bedside gallery offers a glimpse of the hotel's history interspersed with photographs of the celebrities of yesteryear.
2 | British racing green: The color of choice for English sports cars gives this desk a sophisticated elegance.

1 | Schwarz-Weiß: Eine kleine Bildergalerie über dem Bett mixt die Historie des Hauses und Fotos der Prominenz von gestern.
2 | British racing green: Was für englische Sportwagen perfekt ist, kann auch für Schreibtische nicht schlecht sein.

THE BRIEF

History and the spirit of renewal have a unique and tangible presence in Hamburg's old warehouse district. And the "VLET" restaurant is right in the thick of it. The challenge: To create a design that draws on the Speicherstadt's architectural traditions without being constrained by history.

CONCEPT

Brickwork meets haute cuisine – the main contrast is underscored by a complementary contrast. The color green represents freshness and naturalness, qualities that were essential to this project.

AUFGABE

An kaum einem anderen Ort in Deutschland werden Geschichte und Aufbruch so erlebbar wie in Hamburgs Speicherstadt. Mittendrin: Das Restaurant „VLET". Die Herausforderung: Die regionalen Besonderheiten der Speicherstadt für die Gestaltung nutzen, ohne in Historie zu erstarren.

KONZEPT

Backstein trifft auf feine Küchenkunst. Diesen Kontrast gilt es noch zu verstärken – mit einem weiteren: dem Komplementärkontrast. Da die Farbe Grün für Frische und Natürlichkeit steht, darf sie hier nicht fehlen.

RESTAURANT „VLET" | HAMBURG

CATEGORY | KATEGORIE
Fine dining restaurant | Gourmetrestaurant

THE BRIEF | AUFGABE
Creation of a new restaurant in an
old warehouse building | Einbau eines
Restaurants in einen alten Speicher

SIZE | GRÖSSE
390 m²

PROJECT COMPLETED IN | BAUJAHR
2008

COMPLETION PERIOD | BAUZEIT
3 months | 3 Monate

150_3

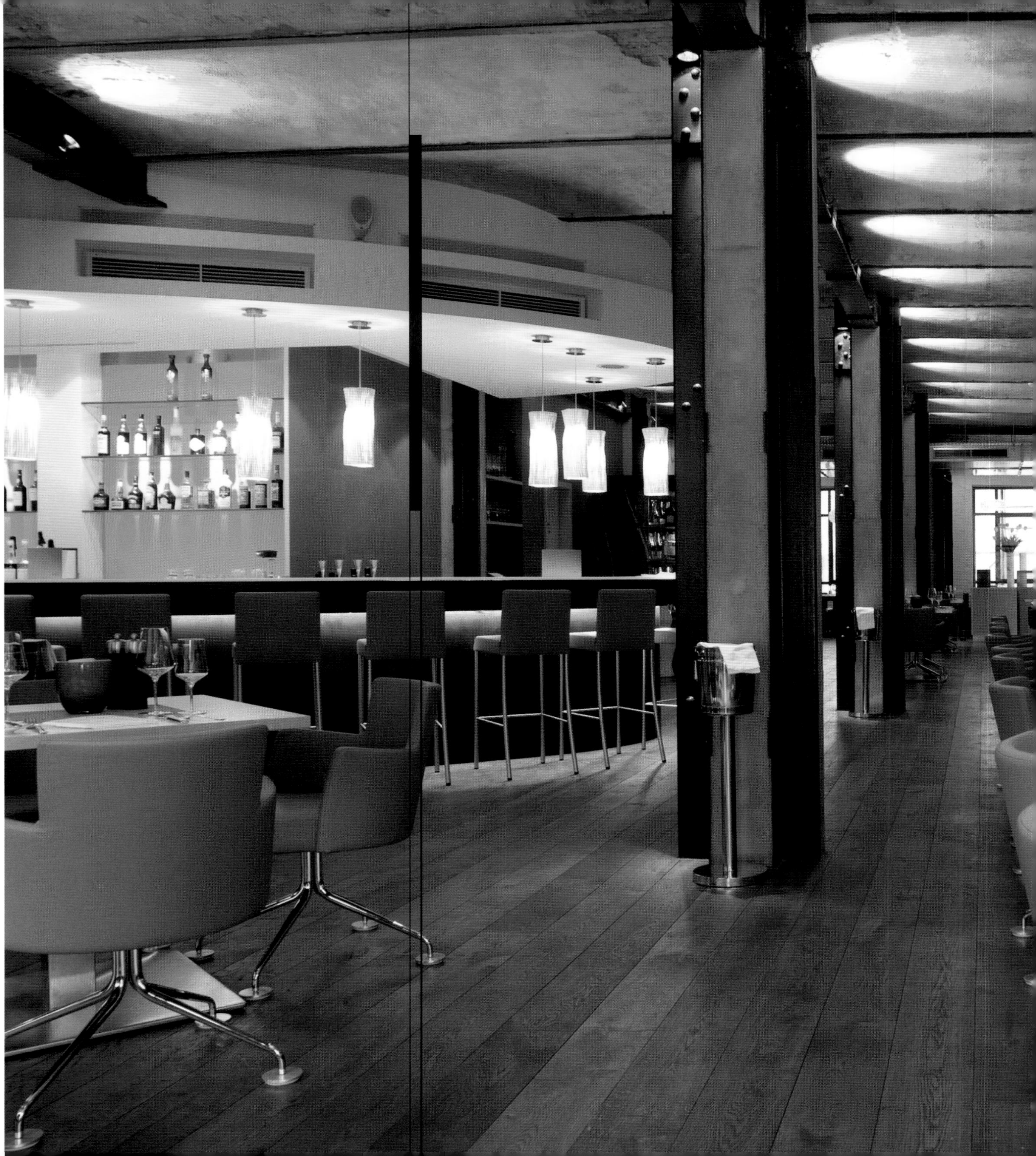

Hanseatic: The location sets the tone for the design of the restaurant and the kitchen. The rustic structure of the bare brick walls and massive steel girders is reflected in the metallic mesh partitions. The exquisite leather upholstery and glamorous chandelier form a strong visual counterpoint.

Hanseatisch: Der Charakter des Restaurants und der Küche hängt unmittelbar mit dem Standort zusammen. Rustikale Strukturen der aufwändig gereinigten Wände aus Backstein und der massiven Stahlstützen wiederholen sich in metallenen Gittergeflechten. Edle Lederpolster und glamouröse Kronleuchter halten dagegen.

RESTAURANT „VLET" | HAMBURG

RESTAURANT „VLET" | HAMBURG

Grünglas:
Der begehbare
Weinschrank
schimmert in
sanftem Grün.

Green glass:
The walk-in wine
cooler exudes a
soft green glow.

154_3

RESTAURANT „VLET" | HAMBURG

Durch eine ausgefeilte Lichttechnik
und warme Farben wird das Restaurant
zu einer attraktiven Anlaufstelle für
die „Hafenarbeiter".

The ingenious lighting
and warm colors make
the restaurant an
attractive rendezvous for
modern dockers.

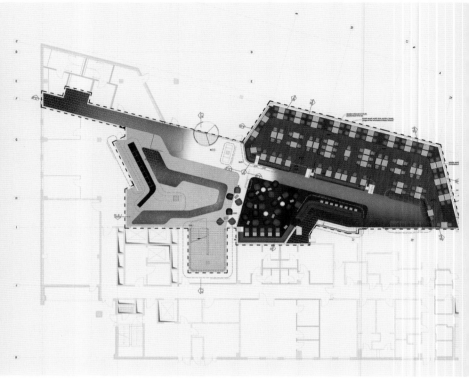

THE BRIEF

The six-story tall Park Inn Krakow offers its guests a remarkable view of the old city of Krakow. The building features a striking façade and form, which offers a stunning horizontal panoramic view. The building's exterior design features dynamic aluminium panelling and dark tinted glass windows. The challenge: To create an interior design that matches the building's eye-catching exterior.

THE CONCEPT

Inside out: The new design transports the powerful visual language of the architecture to the hotel's public areas. The Park Inn Krakow is a young and up-beat four-star quality hotel.

AUFGABE

Das sechsgeschossige Park Inn Krakau eröffnet den Gästen einen außergewöhnlichen Blick auf die Altstadt. Das Gebäude zeichnet sich in seiner Gestalt durch eine ein-prägsame Fassade und Gebäudeform aus, die den horizontalen Panorama-blick aufnimmt. Signifikant ist seine dynamisch gestreifte Aluminium-Fassade mit dunkel getönten Glas-fenstern. Herausforderung: Das innenarchitektonische Konzept sollte dem Äußeren in nichts nachstehen.

KONZEPT

Von Außen nach Innen: Die starke Sprache der Architektur wird in die öffentlichen Bereiche des Hotels transportiert. Das Park Inn Krakau ist ein junges, fröhliches Konzept auf 4-Sterne Niveau.

CATEGORY | KATEGORIE
4*

THE BRIEF | AUFGABE
New hotel construction (public areas and rooms) |
Neubau eines Hotels (Public Areas und Zimmer)

SIZE | GRÖSSE
152 rooms, 2 suites, 8 junior suites |
152 Zimmer, 2 Suiten, 8 Junior Suiten

HOTEL TYPE | HOTEL-TYP
Business/conference hotel | Business-/Konferenzhotel

PROJECT COMPLETED IN | BAUJAHR
2008-09

COMPLETION PERIOD | BAUZEIT
15 months | 15 Monate

ARCHITECTURE/FAÇADE | ARCHITEKTUR/FASSADE
J. Mayer H.

INTERIOR DESIGN |INNENARCHITEKTUR
JOI-Design with Ovotz design Lab. and J. Mayer H. |
JOI-Design mit Ovotz design Lab. und J. Mayer H.

Color follows form: The color composition in the restaurant and bar area exudes a warm and refreshing ambience.

Farbe folgt Form: Der Farbmix im Restaurant und in der Bar vermittelt einen warmen und zugleich frischen Eindruck.

| | | | | | | | | | | | | | | | | | | | | | | | | | | | **PARK INN | KRAKOW | KRAKAU**

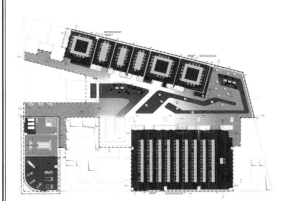

Applied corporate design: The rooms feature the Park Inn brand's four powerful elementary colors – these also feature as accent colors in the hotel's public areas.

Angewandtes Corporate Design: In den Zimmern kommen die vier kräftigen Grundfarben der Marke Park Inn zum Einsatz. In den öffentlichen Bereichen des Hotels tauchen diese Farben als Akzente immer wieder auf.

PARK INN | KRAKOW | KRAKAU

DESIGN.INTERVIEWS_GESPRÄCHS.RAUM

Every day a new
city, every day a
new hotel. Artists
are frequent
travellers and hotel
connoisseurs.
How do they feel
about travelling?
What suggestions
do they have for
hotel managers?

Jeden Tag eine andere Stadt. Jeden Tag ein anderes
Hotel. Künstler sind Vielreisende und daher Hotelexperten.
Wie denken sie über das Reisen? Was empfehlen sie
Hoteldirektoren?

Musician Ingo Pohlmann was born in Rheda-Wiedenbrück
in 1972. He is the founder of "Rocker vom Hocker", an
informal open-mic event for musicians that takes place on
the first Wednesday of every month in Hamburg.

Der Musiker Ingo
Pohlmann wurde 1972
in Rheda-Wiedenbrück
geboren. In Hamburg
begründete er den
monatlichen Mittwoch-
abend „Rocker vom
Hocker". Zwischen
Tresen, Barhockern und
Gelagen: Eine Open-
Stage für Musiker.

INGO POHLMANN IN BRIEF |
INGO POHLMANN IN KÜRZE

What do you love about travelling?

Dr. Samuel Johnson once said: "The use of travelling is to regulate imagination by reality, and instead of thinking how things may be, to see them as they are." As a musician I travel around Germany a lot, and I love to lean my head against the train window and watch the landscape roll past while I let my thoughts wander. I guess I have the soul of a gypsy.

What is your idea of the perfect "hotel moment"?

Sitting in a hotel room after a show with other musicians always brings back memories of hanging out with friends in my bedroom as a teenager. Only hotels have that effect on me.

What can spoil a hotel stay?

Paying for internet access. It's ridiculous. Internet access should be part of the regular hotel service – just like TV.

What suggestions would you like to make to hotel managers?

Give your guests free internet access! They will thank you for it.

What do you always take with you on your travels?

My guitar.

Was lieben Sie am Reisen?

Dr. Samuel Johnson sagte mal: „Auf Reisen zu gehen bedeutet, die Wirklichkeit mit der Vorstellung auszugleichen und anstatt zu denken, wie die Dinge sein könnten, sie zu sehen, wie sie sind." Als Musiker bin ich innerhalb Deutschlands sehr viel unterwegs, und ich liebe es, meinen Kopf ans rüttelnde Fenster zu lehnen und meinen Gedanken freien Lauf zu lassen, während die Landschaft an mir vorbeizieht. Ich habe wohl eine Zigeunerseele.

Der perfekte Hotelmoment?

Nach einer Show im Zimmer eines Kollegen zu sitzen, wirft einen wieder zurück in die Zeit, als man als Teenager im Kinderzimmer seines Elternhauses saß, um mit Freunden abzuhängen. Das erlebe ich so nur in Hotels.

Was bringt Sie im Hotel auf die Palme?

Wenn ich für den Internetzugang zahlen muss. Das ist geradezu lächerlich und sollte genau wie Fernsehen zum Service gehören.

Was empfehlen Sie Hoteldirektoren?

Schalten Sie den Internetzugang für Ihre Gäste frei. Man wird es Ihnen danken.

Worauf können Sie auf Reisen nicht verzichten bzw. welche Teile müssen immer mit?

Meine Gitarre.

CHRISTOPHER VON DEYLEN
IN BRIEF | CHRISTOPHER VON
DEYLEN IN KÜRZE

Christopher von Deylen
founded the music
project Schiller in 1998.
To date von Deylen has
recorded six albums
together with artists such
as Mike Oldfield,
Thomas D, Sarah
Brightman, Lang Lang
and Xavier Naidoo.
Christopher von Deylen
lives and works in
Berlin.

1998 gründete Christopher von Deylen das Musikprojekt
Schiller. Auf den bisher sechs Schiller-Alben arbeitete
von Deylen unter anderem mit den Künstlern Mike Oldfield,
Thomas D, Sarah Brightman, Lang Lang und Xavier Naidoo
zusammen. Christopher von Deylen lebt und arbeitet in
Berlin.

What do you love about travelling?
The fact that you never know exactly what is going to happen next. Travel allows me to satisfy my curiosity and puts my home life in perspective. It's an inspiring experience.

What is your idea of the perfect "hotel moment"?
Enjoying a cup of tea while observing the comings and goings in the lobby.

What can spoil a hotel stay?
Staff who behave as though their guests were somehow inferior. There's no excuse for that cultivated arrogance, no matter how sophisticated a hotel may be. And why some hotels still have smoking rooms is a mystery to me.

What suggestions would you like to make to hotel managers?
Spend more time with your guests and study their faces. A satisfied guest is easily recognised – and an unsatisfied one, too.

What do you always take with you on your travels?
A short-wave radio, flashlight, iPod and an extension cable (most hotel rooms suffer from a chronic shortage of power sockets).

Was lieben Sie am Reisen?
Dass man nie genau weiß, was passieren wird. Ich kann die Neugier stillen, und das Leben zuhause wird wohltuend relativiert. Am Ende steht immer eine Inspiration.

Der perfekte Hotelmoment?
In Ruhe eine Tasse Tee in der Lobby genießen und dabei das Treiben im Hotel beobachten.

Was bringt Sie im Hotel auf die Palme?
Personal, welches feiner als der Gast sein möchte. Diese gepflegte Arroganz hat auch in guten Häusern nichts zu suchen. Und warum es immer noch Raucherräume gibt, ist mir ein Rätsel.

Was empfehlen Sie Hoteldirektoren?
Sich öfter unter die Gäste des Hauses zu mischen, um sich für deren Gesichtsausdruck zu interessieren. Einen zufriedenen Gast erkennt man sofort – einen unzufriedenen auch.

Worauf können Sie auf Reisen nicht verzichten bzw. welche Teile müssen immer mit?
Weltempfänger, Taschenlampe, iPod, Verlängerungskabel (wegen des latenten Steckdosenmangels in den meisten Zimmern).

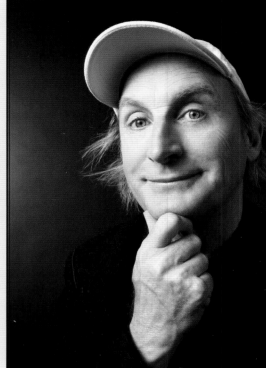

Otto Waalkes was born
in Emden in 1948.
His extraordinary
success story began
in August 1973. In
1985 "Otto – the
Movie" sold a record-
breaking 14.5 million
tickets, making it the
most successful
German film to date.

Otto Waalkes wurde 1948 in Emden
geboren. Ab August 1973 begann
eine einzigartige Erfolgsgeschichte.
„Otto – der Film" bricht mit über 14,5
Millionen Zuschauern 1985 sämtliche
gesamtdeutschen Zuschauerrekorde
und hält sie bis heute.

OTTO WAALKES IN BRIEF |
OTTO WAALKES IN KÜRZE

What do you love about travelling?
I travel so much that I actually rather enjoy just staying at home – but I do still like to travel.

What is your idea of the perfect "hotel moment"?
A cup of hot chocolate at the bar after a performance.

What can spoil a hotel stay?
Nothing can shock me anymore – I've seen it all... even a hotel fire!

What suggestions would you like to make to hotel managers?
Show all of your guests the same degree of courtesy. And don't start by whipping out the visitors' book for the sweaty new arrival to sign.

What do you always take with you on your travels?
I prefer to travel as lightly as possible – which is only possible when a hotel has everything you need.

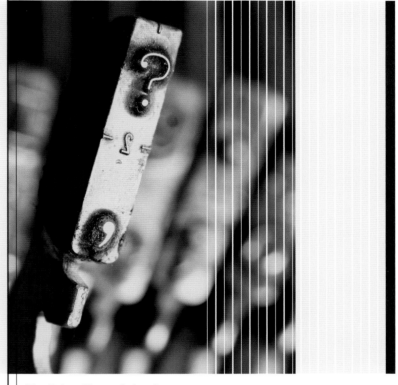

Was lieben Sie am Reisen?
Ich bin so viel auf Reisen, dass ich es noch liebenswerter finde, daheim zu sein – aber ich reise trotzdem gern.

Der perfekte Hotelmoment?
Nach einem Auftritt in die Bar zu kommen und einen heißen Kakao zu kriegen.

Was bringt Sie im Hotel auf die Palme?
Nichts mehr – ich habe schon alles erlebt, bis hin zum Hotelbrand.

Was empfehlen Sie Hoteldirektoren?
Zu allen Gästen gleich freundlich zu sein und nicht als allererstes das Gästebuch zu zücken, in dem man sich dann mit klammen Fingern sofort verewigen soll.

Worauf können Sie auf Reisen nicht verzichten bzw. welche Teile müssen immer mit?
Am schönsten ist es, mit leichtestem Gepäck zu reisen, was voraussetzt, dass im Hotel schon alles da ist.

Was macht ein Hotel zu einem Renner?
Kriterien wie Freundlichkeit, Service, Sauberkeit und Lage haben selbstverständlich immer einen hohen Stellenwert bei erfolgreichen Hotelkonzepten. Vor allem aber ist eine klare Positionierung eines Hauses heute unerlässlich. Durch die steigende Mobilität der Gesellschaft werden zudem Multimedia-Ausstattung und offen gestaltete Gastronomie- und Lobbyflächen für interaktive Aufenthalte immer wichtiger.

▌CHRISTIAN BÖLL IN BRIEF ▐
CHRISTIAN BÖLL IN KÜRZE

Christian Böll, Managing Director of Arabella Hospitality and Managing Director of Arabella-Starwood Hotels & Resorts.

Christian Böll (MBA) trained in Nuremberg, Naples and Ravensburg, and is an expert on hospitality and tourism. As Vice President of Marketing, Christian Böll was responsible for the development and positioning of cruise industry brands AIDA and A-ROSA.

Christian Böll, Geschäftsführer Arabella Hospitality GmbH & Co. KG und Geschäftsführer ArabellaStarwood Hotels & Resorts GmbH

Seine Ausbildung absolvierte der Diplom-Betriebswirt in Nürnberg, Naples und Ravensburg. In seiner Karriere verantwortete der ausgewiesene Hotel- und Tourismusexperte u.a. als Vice President Marketing den Aufbau und die Positionierung der Kreuzfahrtmarken AIDA und A-ROSA.

What makes a hotel successful?
Criteria such as friendliness, service, tidiness and location all contribute to the success of a hotel concept. But above all else, a contemporary hotel must be clearly positioned if it is to succeed. The increasing mobility of our society is paralleled by an increased demand for multimedia facilities, as well as restaurant and lobby areas designed to facilitate interaction.

Was bedeutet für Sie Design?
Hoteldesign sollte außergewöhnlich, aber nicht kompliziert sein. Design und Stil sollten nicht mehr Priorität als Funktionalität, Logistik und Wohlfühlambiente haben. Beide Seiten müssen aufeinander abgestimmt sein und miteinander funktionieren.

What does design mean for you?
Hotel design should be unique, but uncomplicated. Design and style should not take priority over functionality, logistics and the cultivation of a warm atmosphere. A sensitive balance has to be struck between these two aspects of hotel design.

What aspects of the hospitality industry annoy you?
If you aren't passionate about hospitality and serving others, then you are in the wrong business. There's only one thing that I don't like and that is when businesses fail to apply basic principles. When, for instance, hotels neglect to provide further training or product seminars for their staff, when they use standardised procedures and approaches to deal with customers, or when they ignore their guests' wishes.

Where does the future lie for the hospitality industry?
The hospitality industry is set to enjoy continued growth in our increasingly mobile society. The importance of factors such as individuality, consistent quality, brand standards, interactive communication, and a modern and functional design will also continue to grow. In future people will spend more time away from their homes as the boundaries between work and free time dissolve. Hotel concepts will need to be more flexible and able to adapt more rapidly to the needs of tomorrow's travellers.

Was stört Sie am meisten an der Branche?
Entweder man liebt die Hotellerie und den Servicegedanken, oder man ist in der falschen Branche. Deshalb gibt es eigentlich nur eine Sache, die mich stört – wenn die Grundprinzipien nicht umgesetzt werden. Und das ist der Fall, wenn Weiterbildung oder Service- und Produktschulungen vernachlässigt werden oder Standardkonzepte und Massenabfertigung angeboten und Gästebedürfnisse ignoriert werden.

Wo liegt die Zukunft der Hotellerie?
In einer zunehmend mobileren Gesellschaft wird die Hotellerie stets wachsen. Werte wie Individualität, konstante Qualität und Markenstandard, interaktive Kommunikation sowie modern und funktional geplante Hotels werden immer wichtiger. Hotelkonzepte müssen schneller und flexibler an die Bedürfnisse der Reisenden angepasst werden, da zukünftig mehr Zeit außerhalb des Eigenheims verbracht wird und die Grenzen zwischen Beruf und Freizeit miteinander verschmelzen.

J. GEORG KECK IN BRIEF | J. GEORG KECK IN KÜRZE

J. Georg Keck, General Manager Le Méridien Parkhotel Frankfurt und Area General Manager Germany & Russia, Starwood Hotels & Resorts

Following his professional training in Bad Wildbad, J. Georg Keck held a number of international positions, including that of General Manager for Forte in Liège, Amsterdam and Nuremberg. Le Méridien Hotels were first acquired by the Forte Group, and most recently – in November 2005 – by Starwood Hotels & Resorts.

J. Georg Keck, General Manager Le Méridien Parkhotel Frankfurt und Area General Manager Germany & Russia, Starwood Hotels & Resorts

Nach seiner Ausbildung in Bad Wildbad folgten verschiedene internationale Positionen u.a. als General Manager für Forte in Lüttich, Amsterdam und Nürnberg. Nach der Übernahme der Le Méridien Hotels durch Forte folgte im November 2005 die Eingliederung in die Starwood Hotels & Resorts.

What makes a hotel successful?
Trained staff with a positive
outlook, quality service across the
board and the right atmosphere.

What does design mean for you?
Lifestyle.

**What aspects of the hospitality
industry annoy you?**
A lack of commitment to serve.

**Where does the future lie for the
hotel industry?**
In creativity, imagination and
"thinking outside the box".

**Was macht ein Hotel zu
einem Renner?**
Geschultes und positives Personal,
Qualität in allen Bereichen sowie das
richtige Ambiente.

Was bedeutet für Sie Design?
Lifestyle.

**Was stört Sie am meisten
an der Branche?**
Ein Mangel an Dienstleistungs-
bereitschaft.

**Wo liegt die Zukunft der
Hotellerie?**
In mehr Kreativität, Phantasie und
„thinking outside the box".

Was macht ein Hotel zu einem Renner?

1. Die Marke: Ohne klare Positionierung bzw. Identität wird es schwierig.
2. Die Lage: Wohlklingende Adressen lassen die Gäste schon vorher träumen.
3. Die Mundpropaganda: Weitersagen ist wichtig.
4. Der Preis: Wird immer heißer.
5. Das Preis-Leistungsverhältnis: Sollte stimmen.
6. Der Komfort: Ankommen und Wohlfühlen – klingt so einfach, ist aber oft schwierig.
7. Ein Schwimmbad: 1972 bauten wir das Hallenbad im Bristol Hotel Kempinski Berlin. Davon hörte Herbert von Karajan, der stets im Savoy abstieg. Er kam, sah und zog um. Seinem Rücken tat es gut.
8. Die Einrichtung: Oft kann mit geringen Mitteln eine Wohnatmosphäre geschaffen werden, die zum Wiederkommen anregt.
9. Der Service: Freundlichkeit, Zuvorkommenheit und Aufmerksamkeit kosten kein Geld.

Was bedeutet für Sie Design?

Die Kunst der Architekten und Innenarchitekten ist es, dem Hotel eine Identität, einen Wiedererkennungswert und – wenn möglich – Lokalkolorit zu geben. Aber Hand aufs Herz: Ich ziehe Hotelzimmer vor, die mich ausruhen lassen und nicht aufregen und gemütlich sind.

What makes a hotel successful?

1. The brand: A hotel that is not clearly positioned will have a hard furrow to plough.
2. The location: A pleasant-sounding address will fire your guests' imagination before they even arrive.
3. The grapevine: Word of mouth recommendations are important.
4. The price: This is an increasingly important factor.
5. Value for money: You have to get that right.
6. Comfort: Check in and relax – it sounds so easy, but more often than not it isn't.
7. A swimming pool: In 1972 we installed an indoor swimming pool at the Bristol Hotel Kempinski Berlin. When Herbert von Karajan, who always stayed at the Savoy, heard about our swimming pool, he dropped by to have a look, then switched hotels. It was good for his back...
8. The furnishings: It's possible to create an atmosphere that will inspire your guests to return, even with limited resources.
9. The service: A friendly, courteous and attentive manner won' t cost you a cent.

Was stört Sie am meisten an der Branche?

Dass bei Ankunft der Empfang nicht mich anschaut sondern seinen Computer. Dass viele Hotelchefs mehr Zeit hinter dem Schreibtisch verbringen als davor. Dass die Oberkellner fehlen, die den Service trainieren. Dass Kellner Tellerträger geworden sind und verlernt haben zu tranchieren, vorzulegen etc. Dass Investoren an der falschen Stelle sparen. Dass Architekten meist nicht auf die künftigen Betreiber hören und ihren eigenen Gusto und Stil durchsetzen. Dass zu viel rationalisiert wird. Hotels sind keine Fabriken, sondern lebendiger Ausdruck unserer Kultur.

What does design mean for you?

Architects and interior designers are masters in the art of forging an identity, creating recognition value and – where possible – adding local character to a hotel. But I have to admit that I prefer cosy and relaxing hotel rooms to more exciting designs.

What aspects of the hospitality industry annoy you?

The fact that receptionists are more likely to look at their computers than at their new guests. Hotel managers who spend more time behind their desks than in front of them. The dearth of head waiters available to train service. Not to mention that waiters are now less versatile than they once were – many are unable to carve or serve dishes properly. Investors saving money at the wrong end. And architects who refuse to listen to hotel operators, instead following ideas that merely reflect their own tastes. There is too much rationalization in the hotel industry. Hotels are a living and vibrant expression of our culture, they are not factories.

Where does the future lie for the hospitality industry?

1. In the globalisation and liberalisation of human relations. Interest in travel will continue to grow, and markets such as Asia, Arabia, South America and Africa will be further developed.
2. In the construction of modern hotels operated by large hotel groups.
3. In variety, creativity, curiosity, and the pursuit of profit.
4. In the professional training of young people and the development of jobs that are both interesting and useful.
5. In cooperation with people who are committed to progress and creativity.

Born in Berlin in 1934, Rudolf Münster was the Managing Director of M. Kempinski & Co. from 1968 to 1980, and sat on the Board of Directors of Kempinski Hotels AG for seven years. In 1980 he founded RWM Hotel Consult Rudolf W. Münster. He lives in Berlin and Schönau am Königssee.

Der 1934 in Berlin geborene Rudolf Münster war von 1968 bis 1980 Geschäftsführer der M. Kempinski & Co. KG und sieben Jahre Mitglied des Vorstandes der Kempinski Hotels AG. 1980 gründete er die RWM Hotel Consult Rudolf W. Münster GmbH. Er lebt in Berlin und in Schönau am Königssee.

Wo liegt die Zukunft der Hotellerie?

1. In der Globalisierung und Liberalisierung der Menschheit. Die Reiselust wird weiter zunehmen und Märkte wie Asien, Arabien, Südamerika und Afrika werden weiter erschlossen.
2. In der Errichtung neuzeitiger Hotels, betrieben von großen Hotelgesellschaften.
3. In der Vielfalt, der Kreativität, dem Gewinnstreben und der Neugier.
4. In der professionellen Ausbildung junger Menschen und in der Entwicklung von Arbeitsplätzen, die spannend sind und dem Menschen nützen.
5. In der Zusammenarbeit mit Menschen, die sich dem Fortschritt und der Kreativität verschrieben haben.

█ RUDOLF MÜNSTER IN BRIEF | RUDOLF MÜNSTER IN KÜRZE

Karl J. Pojer,
Group Executive Management
TUI Hotels & Resorts, TUI AG

Karl J. Pojer was born in Austria.
Following his school education, he
studied Hotel Management in Austria
and the USA. Pojer is an experienced
diplomat and a former Austrian
consul. In 2006 he was appointed
to the Group Executive Management
of TUI Hotels & Resorts, TUI AG.

Karl J. Pojer,
Bereichsvorstand TUI
Hotels & Resorts,
TUI AG

Der gebürtige Österreicher
absolvierte nach seiner
schulischen Ausbildung ein
mehrjähriges Hotelfach-
studium in Österreich und
später dann in den USA.
Erfahrungen im diplo-
matischen Dienst erwarb
Karl J. Pojer als Konsul
von Österreich. 2006
wurde er zum Bereichs-
vorstand TUI Hotels &
Resorts bei der
TUI AG ernannt.

What makes a hotel successful?
There are a number of factors, but
it is primarily a question of location
and product, ability to reach your
target group, hardware, guest and
employee satisfaction, and effective
management. The focus has to be on
people – your guests and your staff.
You have to exceed your guests'
expectations. Hotels also need
to create a warm atmosphere that
communicates an aura of personalised
service to their guests.

What does design mean for you?
Design should be "quiet" and smart,
not loud and extravagant. Design
should lead to the creation of a
pleasant and inspiring environment
with a positive atmosphere – an
atmosphere that stimulates our visual,
aural and, increasingly, our olfactory
senses. In a nutshell: Design should
be based on people and their
manifold needs.

KARL J. POJER IN BRIEF | KARL J. POJER IN KÜRZE

What aspects of the hospitality industry annoy you?

Hotels that try to please everyone and every target group. The brand confusion displayed by some business hotel chains. The uncoordinated development of new holiday standards and destinations. The construction of more and more hotels without any regard to their sustainability, and the tendency of many hoteliers to follow every trend. All too often hoteliers simply copy their competitor's services and products – people reconcile themselves to their own mediocrity instead of daring to create a specialised niche. Sadly, our industry is also afflicted by this tendency.

Where does the future lie for the hospitality industry?

If the hospitality industry succeeds in making the extraordinary its standard, then standards may improve. The industry needs to counteract the constant acceleration of our everyday lives with a strategy of deceleration based on individuality, quality and strong design concepts. Authentic and sustainable development will become more important, and artificial resorts will face a steady decline. There will be sufficient guest potential to service all industry segments from budget to luxury.

Was macht ein Hotel zu einem Renner?

Neben vielen einzelnen Faktoren ist es die Mixtur aus Standort, Produkt, Zielgruppenansprache, Hardware, Gäste- und Mitarbeiterzufriedenheit sowie Betriebswirtschaftlichkeit. Der Mensch – ob Gast oder Mitarbeiter – muss dabei im Mittelpunkt des Handelns stehen. Der Gast muss verblüfft werden. Und das Hotel muss eine Wohlfühlatmosphäre erzeugen, die der Gast als eine auf seine individuellen Bedürfnisse abgestellte Serviceleistung empfinden kann.

Was bedeutet für Sie Design?

Design mag ich lieber leise und smart als laut und schrill. Design sollte in einer sympathischen und anregenden Gestaltung enden und eine positive Atmosphäre schaffen. Diese gestalterische Atmosphäre wird vor allem geprägt durch optische Reize, durch Licht, durch Akustik und zunehmend auch durch Gerüche. Kurzum: Design soll sich an Menschen und deren vielfältigen Bedürfnissen orientieren.

Was stört Sie am meisten an der Branche?

Hotels, die versuchen, jedem Gast und jeder Zielgruppe gerecht zu werden. Die Markenkonfusion mancher Businesshotelketten. Die unkoordinierte Entwicklung von neuen Urlaubsstandorten und -zielen. Der unkontrollierte Bauboom ohne Rücksicht auf Nachhaltigkeit ebenso wie der Wahn, auf jeden Trend aufzuspringen. Leistungen, Angebote werden zu oft kopiert – die schmerzfreie Akzeptanz von Mittelmäßigkeit gegenüber der Möglichkeit, sich durch Spezialisierung qualitativ im Markt abzugrenzen, ist eine bedauernswerte Entwicklung, auch in unserer Branche.

Wo liegt die Zukunft der Hotellerie?

Wenn es der Hotellerie gelingt, dass das Besondere normal wird, hat das Normale die Chance, besser zu werden. Der täglichen Beschleunigung des Lebens muss die Hotellerie durch gute Konzepte, Individualität und Qualität eine Entschleunigung gegenüber stellen. Authentische, nachhaltige Entwicklungen werden einen noch höheren Stellenwert erhalten, künstliche Resorts werden sich überleben. Von Budget bis Luxus wird es auch in Zukunft genügend Gästepotenzial geben.

UNREALISED.DESIGNS_ABSTELL.RAUM_178_5

Entwurfe, die nicht realisiert wurden, aber dennoch für sich sprechen. Willkommen im Abstell.Raum.

Designs that were
never realised but
nonetheless speak
for themselves.
Welcome to
Unrealised. Designs.

AUFGABE

Aus einer ehemaligen Prager Klinik sollte ein mondänes Hotel entstehen. Das Gelände liegt nur einen Steinwurf von der Moldau entfernt.

IDEE

Die regionalen Besonderheiten fließen in das Konzept mit ein. So dienen die Wellenbewegungen der Moldau als verbindendes gestalterisches Element.

THE BRIEF

We were commissioned to convert a former medical center into a sophisticated hotel. The site was just a stone's throw from the Vltava River.

THE IDEA

Distinctive regional characteristics were integrated into the design concept, which draws on the motif of water movement in the Vltava River to link the individual design elements.

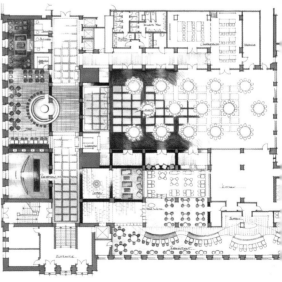

Art Nouveau 2.0: A modern
interpretation of Prague's Jugendstil
designs was developed for the rooms.
Ornamental elements were used
sparingly. The look: elegant,
warm, decorous.

Jugendstil 2.0: Für die Zimmer wurde eine moderne
Übersetzung des in Prag sehr verbreiteten Jugendstils
gefunden. Ornamente werden als Stilmittel zurückhaltend
eingesetzt. Die Optik: elegant, warm, gediegen.

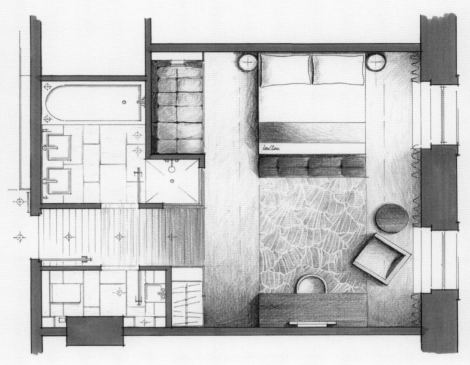

RIVER LOUNGE HOTEL | PRAGUE | PRAG

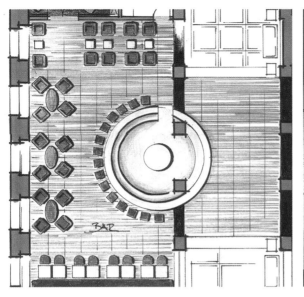

1 | Kristallklar: In der Bar dreht sich alles um Kristall. Eine Verneigung vor der großen tschechischen Glasbläserkunst.
2 | Gold in der Goldenen Stadt: Der offene Empfangsbereich mit geschwungener, goldfarbener Wand.

1 | Crystal clear: At the bar it's all about the crystal. The bar is an homage to the artistry of Czech glassblowing.
2 | Gold in the Golden City: The open reception area is enhanced by the sweeping curve of a golden wall.

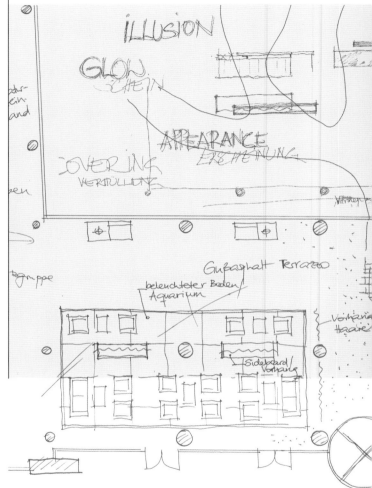

THE BRIEF

Our task was to create a design for a hotel located on the banks of the Rhine.

THE IDEA

The view: Inspired by the close proximity of the legendary Lorelei rock, the design has an enchanting and playful character.

AUFGABE

Neuentwicklung eines Hotels, das direkt am Rhein liegt.

IDEE

Dieser Blick: Da die Lorelei nicht weit ist, haben die Entwürfe etwas Märchenhaftes, Spielerisches an sich.

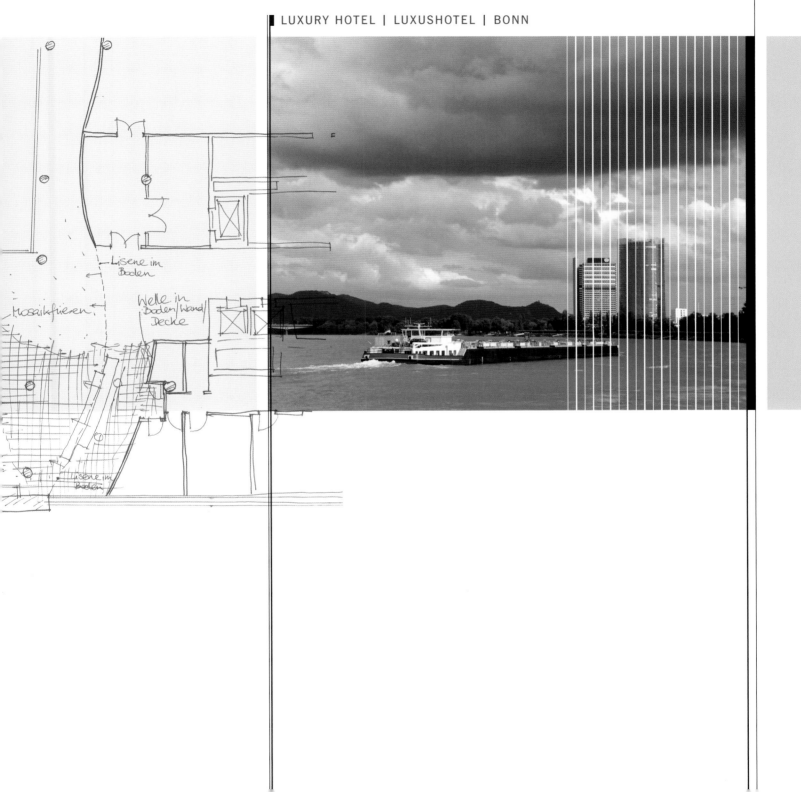

Lisene im Boden

Mosaikfriesen

Welle in Boden/Wand/Decke

Lisene im Boden

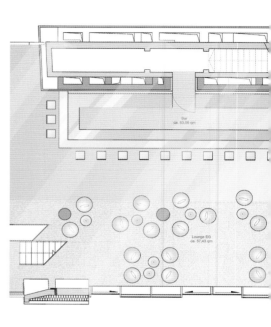

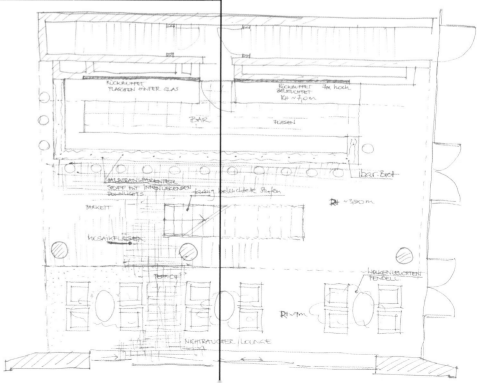

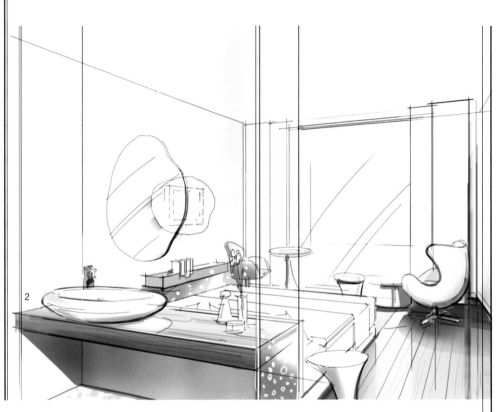

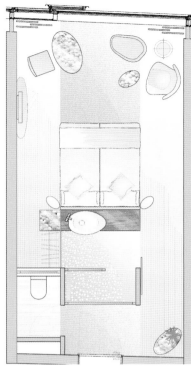

1 | Slide on down to the bar: More adventurous guests can take the slide to the bar. The bar area is illuminated by a distinctive lighting fixture that resembles a cloud.
2 | All angles covered: Guests enjoy direct views of the Rhine from their beds and from the wash basin, which is separated from the bedroom by a glass wall.

1 | Stufenlos zur Bar: Über eine Rutsche gelangt der Gast – wenn er möchte – an die Bar. Für lichte Verhältnisse sorgen die Leuchtkörper in Form einer Wolke.
2 | Alles im Blick: Das Bett ist so platziert, dass der Gast den direkten Blick auf den Rhein hat. Ebenso das Waschbecken, das durch eine Glasscheibe vom Bett getrennt ist.

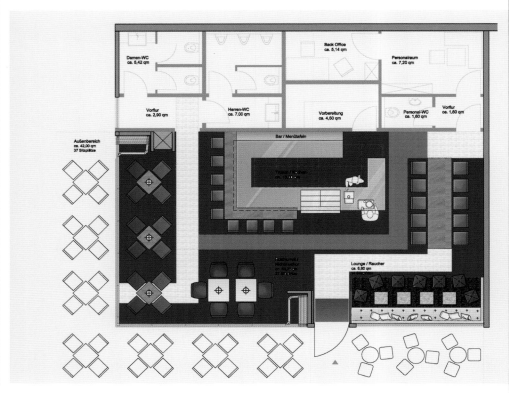

THE BRIEF
To develop a design concept for an Italian cafe.

THE IDEA
Buono: Experience the luxurious side of Italy. Classical elements were combined with new forms and materials to create this contemporary interpretation.

AUFGABE
Entwicklung eines Konzeptes für eine italienische Kaffeebar.

IDEE
Buono: Italien erleben und auf hohem Niveau genießen. Klassische Elemente werden mit neuen Formen und Materialien kombiniert und so zeit-gemäß interpretiert.

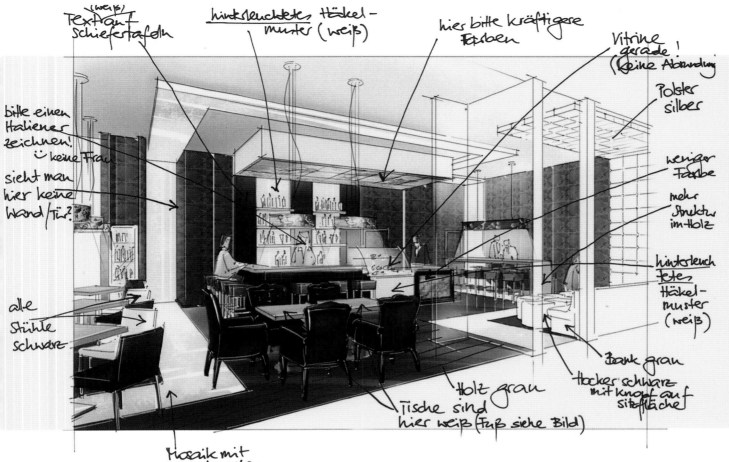

Text auf (weiß)
Schiefertafeln

hinterleuchtetes Häkel-
muster (weiß)

hier bitte kräftigere
Farben

Vitrine
gerade!
(keine Abrundung)

Polster
silber

bitte einen
Italiener
zeichnen!
i keine Frau

sieht man
hier keine
Wand/Tür?

weniger
Farbe

mehr
Struktur
im Holz

hinterleuch-
tetes
Häkel-
muster
(weiß)

alle
Stühle
schwarz

Bank grau

Holz grau

Hocker schwarz
mit Knopf auf
Sitzfläche

Tische sind
hier weiß (Fuß siehe Bild)

Mosaik mit
Barockmuster

CAFÉ-BAR CONCEPT | CAFÉ-BAR KONZEPT

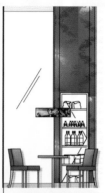

Alles unter Kontrolle: Der Barrista bildet das Zentrum des Raumes. Der Barbereich ist in verschiedene Zonen aufgeteilt und kann flexibel genutzt werden.

Everything under control: The barista is the centerplace of the room. The bar area is divided into a number of zones and is designed for multi-purpose use.

DOLCE HOTEL | BRUSSELS | BRÜSSEL

THE BRIEF
We were commissioned
to convert a former
IBM training center in
Brussels into a modern
conference hotel.

THE IDEA
The external
features have, in strict
accordance with feng
shui principles, been
taken indoors.

AUFGABE
Aus dem ehemaligen IBM-
Schulungszentrum in Brüssel
sollte ein modernes Tagungs-
hotel werden.

IDEE
Das Äußere wird, streng nach
Feng Shui, nach innen geholt.

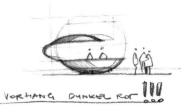

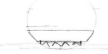

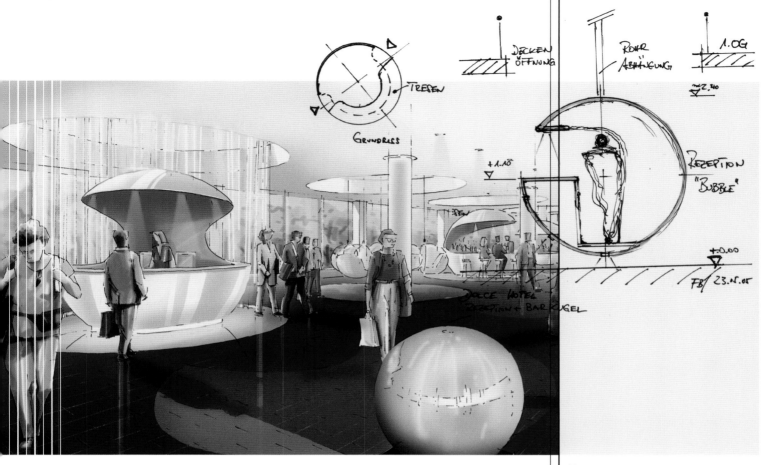

DECKEN ÖFFNUNG

ROHR ABHÄNGUNG

1.OG

TRESEN

GRUNDRISS

~2.40

+1.10

REZEPTION "BUBBLE"

+0.00

FB/ 23.05.05

DOLCE HOTEL
REZEPTION + BAR KUGEL

Elementarteilchen: In der Lobby
dienen einzelne Atome des Brüsseler
Atomiums als Inspirationsquelle.

Atomized: The stylized atoms
of Brussels' Atomium inspired
the design of the lobby.

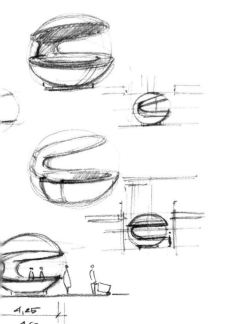

4,25

4,50

DOLCE HOTEL | BRUSSELS | BRÜSSEL

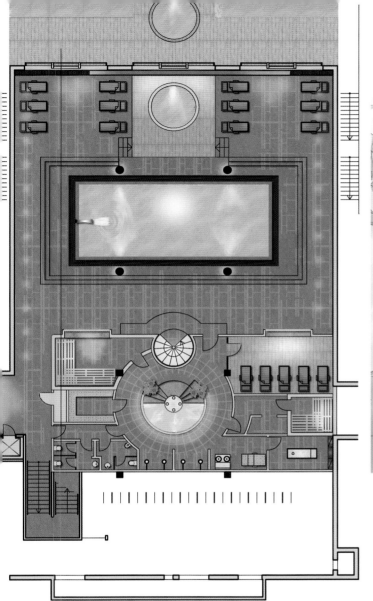

Wasser marsch: Der Wellnessbereich ist in zwei Ebenen unterteilt. Die untere Ebene widmet sich komplett dem Element Wasser. Gemäß der Lehre Feng Shui fließt das Wasser zum Gebäude hin; es erhält dadurch positive Energie.

Go with the flow: The wellness area is comprised of two levels. Water dominates the design of the lower level. The water flows towards the building – according to the principles of Feng Shui this charges the building with positive energy.

DOLCE HOTEL | BRUSSELS | BRÜSSEL

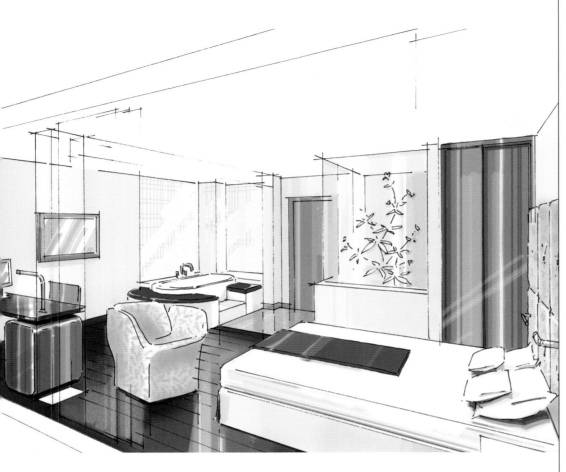

Den Durchblick haben: Die offenen
Zimmergrundrisse setzen den Gedanken
der Verbindung zur Natur fort. Alle
Elemente im Raum sind nach außen
gerichtet. Abgerundete Formen ziehen
sich fließend durch die Zimmer.

Open vistas: The open floor plan of the rooms
emphasises the hotel's natural character. All of the
elements in the rooms face outwards and the rounded
forms of the furnishings flow through the room.

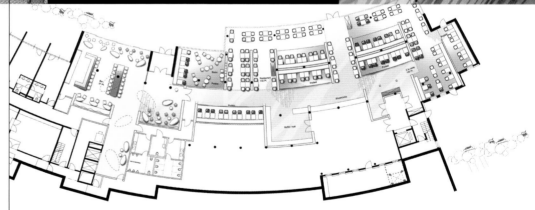

LAKESITE HOTEL | FLEESENSEE

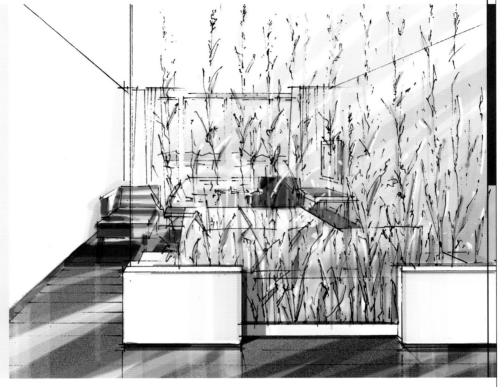

THE BRIEF
To create a design for a lakeside
resort hotel.

THE IDEA
Nature defines the landscape. The
use of grass, bulrushes and wind
communicates a sense of lightness,
motion and an affinity for
the landscape.

AUFGABE
Gestaltung eines Resorthotels direkt am See.

IDEE
Die Natur prägt die Landschaft. Mit Gräsern, Binsen und
Wind wird in den Entwürfen Leichtigkeit, Bewegung und
Erdverbundenheit vermittelt.

An oasis in the East: The motion of grass in the wind is reflected in the intarsias decorating the flooring.

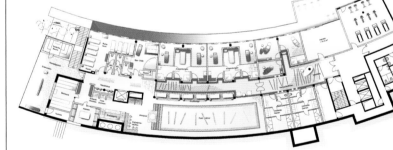

Oase im Osten: Intarsien im Boden spiegeln die Bewegung der Gräser im Wind wider.

NIVEA HOUSE | NIVEA HAUS | HAMBURG

Lager
Paletten 25

Beratung
10-15
EG o OG

259 m²

Kosmetik

THE BRIEF
This design brings the spirit of the Nivea brand to the interiors of Hamburg's Nivea House.

THE IDEA
The design traces the motion of a rolling Nivea tin and transforms the movement into a series of large-scale sculptures. The concept was developed in co-operation with Planungsbüro Deyle.

AUFGABE
Im Hamburger Nivea Haus sollte die Marke erlebbar werden.

IDEE
Die Bewegung einer rollenden Nivea-Dose wird eingefroren, zieht eine Spur durch das Gebäude und wird teilweise zu großen kunstvollen Skulpturen verarbeitet. Das Projekt wurde in Zusammenarbeit mit dem Planungsbüro Deyle konzipiert.

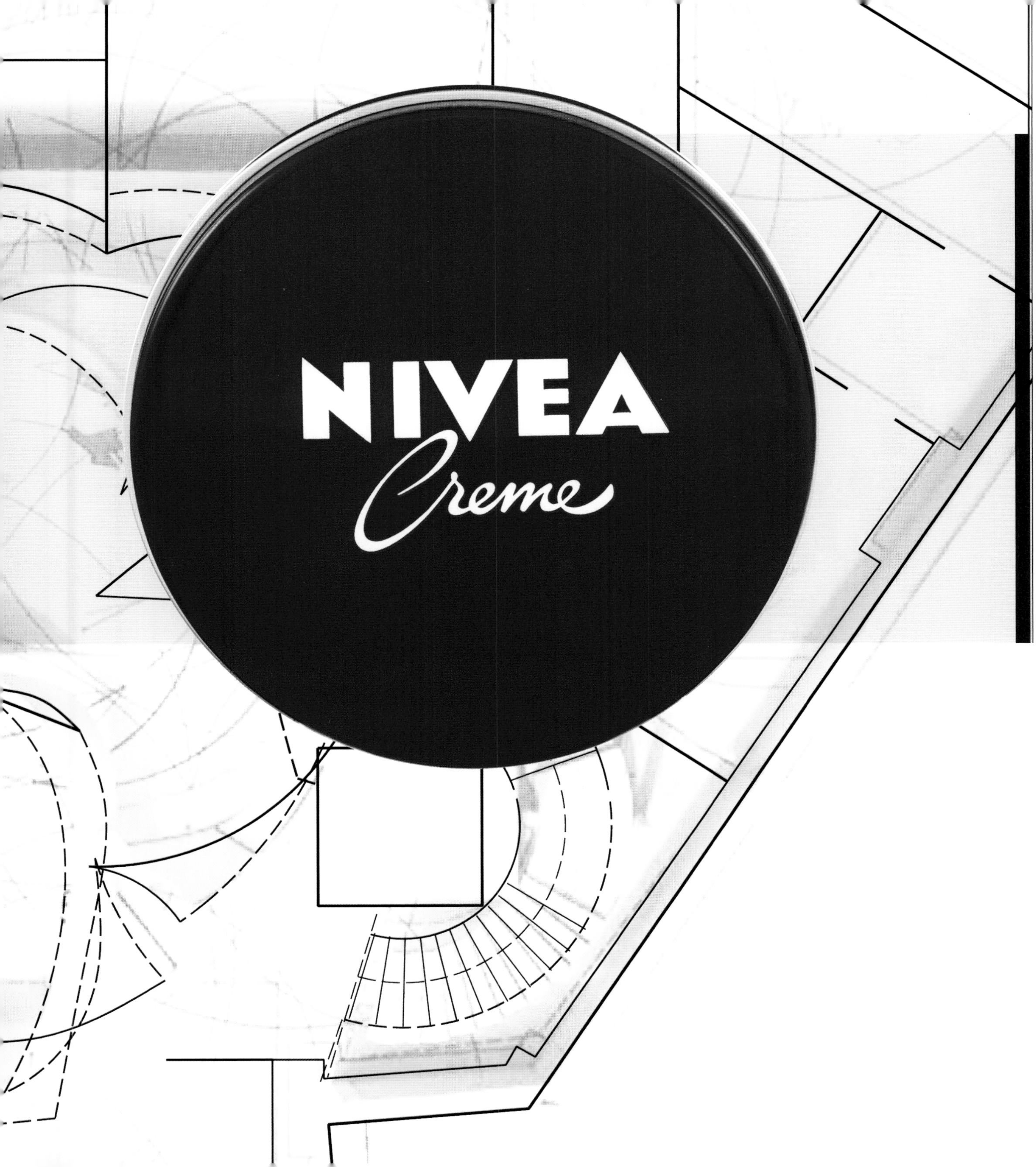
NIVEA
Creme

Bar

Theke
1.10

1.20

2.00

Deckenschirm

Eventfläche

Deckenschirm

Deckenschirm

50 Plätze

UKD
-0.50

Tchibo Lounge

16 Plätze

2.00

Kaffeebar

0.50

Schiebewände

Bank

0.40

Theke
1.10

Empfang

1.40

UKD
-0.20

0.50

6.00

Frozen movement:
The traces of the
Nivea tin's
frozen motion
extends across
three levels.

Frozen movement:
Auf drei Ebenen wird
der Besucher Zeuge
der eingefangenen
Bewegung einer Nivea-
Dose.

IDEAS_IDEEN.RAUM_208_6

Hospitality Design, the philosophy of JOI-Design.

IDEAS IDEEN.RAUM

Hospitality Design wie JOI-Design es sieht.

By Corinna
Kretschmar-Joehnk
and Peter Joehnk.

Von Corinna Kretschmar-
Joehnk und Peter Joehnk.

SEDUCE AND SELL! – THOUGHTS ON HOSPITALITY DESIGN |
VERFÜHREN UND VERKAUFEN! – GEDANKEN ZUM HOSPITALITY DESIGN

Die Currywurst ist ehrlich, geschmackvoll und bodenständig. Sushi ist kunstvoll, akkurat und international. Corinna Kretschmar-Joehnk liebt Sushi und mag Currywurst. Peter Joehnk liebt Currywurst und mag Sushi. In ihrer Arbeit mixen die beiden Innen-architekten gekonnt Gegensätze, denken über Tellerränder hinweg und konzipieren Dinge zu einem geschmackvollen Ganzen.

The currywurst is a fundamentally honest, tasty and down-to-earth snack. Sushi is artistic, precise and inter-national. Corinna Kretschmar-Joehnk loves sushi and likes currywurst. Peter Joehnk loves currywurst and likes sushi. These two talented interior designers are masters in the art of blending contrasting elements, thinking outside the box and creating uniquely stylish designs.

Hospitality Design – the creation of warm and welcoming spaces for guests – has become increasingly important in recent years. Gone are the days when a housekeeper could torpedo a design by insisting that it would take three minutes longer to clean. While white carpeting and piano lacquer still rarely figure in contemporary designs, decision-makers in the hospitality industry have come to understand that hotels are built for guests, not for employees.

But three minutes are still three minutes... And in a 200-room hotel three minutes per room adds up to 600 minutes per day – or one additional cleaner. If the rooms in our hypothetical hotel are renovated every ten years, then those three additional minutes will add up to 36,500 additional working hours over ten years. But filling those rooms with guests is undoubtedly more important than cleaning them. And the hotelier who fails to attract any guests will not have to worry about cleaning ...

Hospitality design is applied marketing

Change is in the air – a change that will see hospitality design become an integral aspect of marketing. In order to ensure smiling faces at the breakfast tables the design must appeal first and foremost to the guests, then to the employees. There is more to Hospitality Design than merely creating a cool atmosphere. It is about developing designs tailor-made to fit the needs of operators, hotel brands, and guest structures. Hospitality design seeks to achieve a correspondence between the brand core and its perception. Hospitality design can be everything and anything, but never dull: theme-oriented, tailor-made for individual cities, down to earth, wild, elegant, distinguished, modern, reserved or sharp. Just as long as it never fails to seduce.

Das Hospitality Design, also all das, was Räume für Gäste schöner und behaglicher machen soll, hat in den letzten Jahren deutlich an Bedeutung gewonnen. Vorbei sind die Zeiten, in denen die Hausdame einen gewagten Entwurf der Innen-architekten mit dem Kommentar kippen konnte, dass sie zum Putzen drei Minuten länger bräuchte. Auch heute werden selten weiße Teppiche und Klavierlack eingesetzt, aber bei den Entscheidern in Hotellerie und Gastronomie hat sich die Erkenntnis durchgesetzt, dass für den Gast und nicht für die Hausdame gebaut wird.

Allerdings bleiben drei Minuten immer noch drei Minuten. Bei 200 Hotelzimmern sind das 600 Minuten am Tag, und das bedeutet eine zu-sätzliche Reinigungskraft. Setzt man den Renovierungsturnus eines Hotel-zimmers mit 10 Jahren an, dann multiplizieren sich die drei Minuten auf 36.500 zusätzliche Stunden. Dennoch: Wichtiger als die Zimmer zu putzen, ist zunächst einmal Gäste in die Zimmer zu bekommen – denn wenn die nicht kommen, braucht auch nicht gereinigt zu werden.

Return on investment in hospitality design

How does this issue impact on the design process? Basically, it requires that designers are cognizant of their target groups, sharply define their profiles, and master communication strategies. Interior designers could learn a lot from advertising agencies with regard to this aspect of their work. The more hotel beds a guest has to choose from, the more important product positioning and communication management will become. At the end of the day, the purpose of hospitality design is to improve a hotel operator's chances of filling their rooms, and to enable investors to make a return on their investment. In a nutshell: The return on hospitality design investments has to be right.

Atmosphere. Individuality. Character.

Hospitality design that doesn't sell doesn't make sense. Some designers and architects like to think of themselves as artists; unfortunately they aren't. Artists enjoy the privilege of being able to give free rein to their creativity. Uninhibited by external influences, artists are accountable to no one but themselves. Architects, interior designers and designers, on the other hand, are given the task of using someone else's money to create a product that will, hopefully, be a success. When designers seek only to make their own ideas reality, they inevitably create cold and unwelcoming rooms that few guests enjoy. Hospitality design is a tool for creating a warm and pleasant atmosphere. The designer's task is to create an atmosphere that suits both the hotel and its guests. The more beds there are on the market – and there are more every day – the more important the task of carving out a distinctive character becomes. What's more: The more responsive a hotel is to the personality of its guests, the greater its success will be. That is how it has always been and how it will probably always be.

Hospitality Design ist angewandtes Marketing

Die Zeichen der Zeit stehen auf Wandel. Ein Wandel, der Hospitality Design als Teil des Marketings begreift. Denn eine Innenarchitektur, die für glückliche Gesichter am Frühstückstisch sorgt, muss zuallererst dem Fisch schmecken und dann dem Angler. Hospitality Design bedeutet nicht nur cooles Ambiente, sondern je nach Betreiber, je nach Hotelmarke und je nach Gästestruktur, das am besten passende Design. Das Fitting ist entscheidend, die Überein-stimmung von Markenkern und avisierter Fremdwahrnehmung. Hospitality Design kann dabei alles sein, nur nicht langweilig: Themenorientiert, stadt-spezifisch, bodenständig, wild, elegant, distinguiert, modern, sachlich, klar. Und wie gesagt: Nur nie nicht verführen.

Return on Hospitality Design Investment

Was bedeutet das für die Arbeit der Gestalter? Im Kern heißt es, Zielgruppen im Blick zu haben, das eigene Profil zu erkennen und zu schärfen und kommunikationsstrategisch durchdacht zu planen. Die Gestalter von Räumen können sich in diesem Zusammenhang viel von der Arbeitsweise der Werbe-agenturen abschauen. Denn je mehr Hotelbetten dem Gast zur Verfügung stehen, desto wichtiger werden eine klare Positionierung und eine perfekt inszenierte Kommunikation. Am Ende des Tages geht es darum, dem Betreiber die Chance auf ein volles Haus zu geben und dem Investor die Chance auf eine Verzinsung seiner Investition zu ermöglichen. Kurzum: Der Return on Hospitality Design Investment muss stimmen.

Atmosphäre. Individualität. Charakter.

Hospitality Design, das nicht verkauft, macht keinen Sinn. Offensichtlich fühlen sich einige Designer und Architekten als Künstler, ohne dies aber wirklich zu sein. Denn Künstler haben das Privileg, ihre Kreativität frei von Zielen und Zwängen anderer auszuüben und sind nur sich selbst Rechen-schaft schuldig. Architekten, Innenarchitekten und Designer schulden ihrem Auftraggeber hingegen ein Werk, welches sie mit fremdem Geld schaffen und das daher möglichst erfolgreich sein sollte. Abgehobene Kopfgeburten führen fast zwangsläufig zu kalten, gefühllosen Räumen, in denen sich Gäste selten wohl fühlen. Hospitality Design aber ist ein Werkzeug, um eine stimmige Raumatmosphäre zu schaffen. Und es hängt am Geschick des Designers, diese Atmosphäre so zu erspüren, dass sie zum Objekt und zum Gast passt. Je mehr Betten da draußen feilgeboten werden – und es werden immer mehr – desto wichtiger wird es, den individuellen Charakter eines Hotels herauszuarbeiten. Und: Je stärker das Hotel auf die Persönlichkeit seiner Gäste eingeht, desto erfolgreicher wird es sein. Das war schon immer so, und das wird wahrschein-lich auch immer so bleiben.

Hospitality design is teamwork.
A look inside the JOI-Design workshop.

Hospitality Design ist Teamwork. Ein
Blick in die Werkstatt von JOI-Design.

1

2

1 | Natural wonders:
The core idea behind the design
of the offices was to create a
connection to nature and the
adjacent canal. The motion of the
water is reflected in the forms,
patterns and colors of the design.
At the heart of the office: The
extensive materials archive where
employees often work with clients to
develop ideas and design concepts.
2 | Sit in style: The red sofa is the
hub of the office.

1 | Naturschauspiel: Die übergreifende Idee bei der Gestaltung des eigenen
Büros ist die Verbindung zur Natur mit dem Fleet vor der Tür. Die Bewegungen
des Wassers spiegeln sich in Formen, Mustern und Farben der Einrichtung
wider. Im Herzen des Büros: Das umfangreiche Materialarchiv, in dem oft
gemeinsam mit Kunden Ideen und Konzepte entwickelt werden.
2 | Sitzen bleiben: Das rote Sofa als Dreh- und Angelpunkt im Büro.

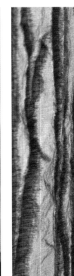

JOI-DESIGN | SPACE FOR DIALOGUE | RAUM FÜR GESPRÄCHE

1 | A strong team: Corinna Kretschmar-Joehnk and Peter Joehnk are inseparable – both in their professional and personal lives. Peter Joehnk in his own words: "Great design is always the result of teamwork"

2 | Water, air and earth: The conference room looks out on the canal.

1 | Beziehungsweise: Corinna Kretschmar-Joehnk und Peter Joehnk – ein Paar im Leben und im Job.
O-Ton Peter Joehnk: „Brillante Konzepte entstehen immer im Team."

2 | Wasser, Luft und Erde: Der Besprechungsraum mit Blick auf den Fleet.

1 | A versatile team: The JOI-team is comprised of interior designers, architects, designers, communication experts, civil engineers, project managers, old hands and young minds.
2 | Material testing: Mood boards are put together in the material room.
3 | Space: The floor layout was designed to facilitate communication between team members. In the picture: the team mascot – our beloved mutt Cittino.

1 | Kopf- und Handarbeit: Das JOI-Team besteht aus Innenarchitekten, Architekten, Designern, Kommunikationsexperten, Bauingenieuren, Projektmanagern, alten Hasen und jungen Kreativen.
2 | Stoffprobe: Moodboards werden im Stoffraum zusammengestellt.
3 | Freiraum: Die Aufteilung der Räume wurde so angelegt, dass die Mitarbeiter problemlos kommunizieren können. Auch im Bild: Das Maskottchen des Büros – Mischlingshund Cittino.

▌PICTURE CREDITS | BILDNACHWEIS

JOI-Design, Peter Joehnk
128, 129, 130, 131, 136, 137, 138, 139

Tobias D. Kern
132, 133, 134, 135

Hotel Kokenhof, Großburgwedel
20, 29

Le Méridien Parkhotel, Frankfurt am Main
63, 172

McCafé
116, 117

Hotel meerSinn, Binz, Rügen
57, 58

Hotel Ritter, Durbach
97, 99, 100, 102, 103, 104, 105, 106, 107, 114, 115

Tanja Schäfer
62

Shutterstock
30, 180, 194

Hotel Steigenberger, Hamburg
73, 75, 77, 78, 79

TUI Hotels & Resorts, TUI AG
176

Elita Wiegand
15

Ben Wolf
164

Z_punkt
15

▌ CONTACT | KONTAKT

JOI-Design GmbH
Innenarchitekten

Medienpark [k]ampnagel
Barmbeker Str. 6a
22303 Hamburg
Germany

Phone: +49 (0) 40 / 68 94 21 - 0
Fax: +49 (0) 40 / 68 94 21 - 30

info@JOI-Design.com
www.JOI-Design.com